Everyday
Resilience

Everyday Resilience

A Practical Guide to Build Inner Strength
and Weather Life's Challenges

GAIL GAZELLE, MD

ROCKRIDGE
PRESS

Interior and Cover Designer: Brieanna Hattey Felschow
Art Producer: Karen Williams
Editors: Seth Schwartz and Nora Spiegel
Production Editor: Ruth Sakata Corley

Photography © Helene Dujardin.
Author photo courtesy of © Ana Matei.

ISBN: Print 978-1-64739-501-8 | eBook 978-1-64739-305-2

R0

To my son, a beacon of light, love, and goodness. And to LG, whose resilience allowed me to heal and move forward from tragedy to wholeness.

Contents

Introduction

Imagine for a moment that you have the resilience of a master. You go through your day able to weather whatever challenges come along. You go through your week, your month, your year confident in your ability to handle all the punches life throws at you. Imagine the circumstances of your life as they are now; what's changed is that you have exactly the resources you need to remain whole, steady, and solid. Reflect on how good this would feel. Take in the sense of mastery and empowerment you'd experience.

I want you to know that this level of mastery is completely within your reach.

Whatever your age or life experience, it's likely that you've experienced your share of challenge and difficulty along the way. Job instability, illness, accidents, loss of an important relationship, even a global pandemic—these events are part of the fabric of what we encounter in this journey we call life. And doesn't it often seem that just when you move through one set of challenges and find stability, another one arises? That, too, is simply the nature of life.

At times you may wonder how you'll cope with the difficulties you face, and whether you'll have the resilience you need when the going gets tough. It's true that resilience gives us the inner resources—courage, strength, wisdom—we require to deal with difficult circumstances. But resilience also provides the realization that how we fare in life has less to do with the particular challenges we experience and more to do with how we respond to those challenges.

It turns out that you already have resilience deep within you. Though we often consider resilience to be an exceptional quality, in fact it resides within every one of us. But most of us don't know how to access our resilience, as we never learned that we each have a deep, unshakeable inner core of strength and capability. For many of us, rediscovering that buried core of resilience takes some thoughtful and determined excavation. That is just the journey on which this book is going to take you.

The tools to manage life's travails and the inner core of strength you need are deep within you right now, waiting to be deployed. Modern neuroscience has revealed much about how we can tap into this core and sharpen those tools. In this book, we'll explore some of these evolving discoveries to deepen your understanding of the capacity for resilience that we all possess.

In my professional life, I've worked with thousands of individuals going through all types of difficult life events. As a hospice physician, I was dedicated to helping those facing the end of their lives. I saw many of these individuals succumb to psychological pain and anguish. And I also saw many people mobilize their inner resources, enabling them to get their affairs in order, say goodbye to those who were most important to them, and spend their remaining time on what they valued.

Fifteen years into my work caring for the terminally ill, the practice of medicine entered a particularly challenging time. The advent of the electronic medical record, increased focus on productivity, and the emphasis on the bottom line left physicians feeling estranged from their calling, depleted and overwhelmed by administrative burdens that kept them from the important task of tending to their patients. I wanted to help and decided to become an executive physician coach. Over the ensuing 10 years, I've had the privilege of coaching over 500 physician colleagues from around North America. In that capacity I've also witnessed the tremendous ability individuals have to work with their own inner core to overcome the difficulties life has put in their path. Along the way I deepened my individual mindfulness practice and became a certified mindfulness meditation instructor.

I also have personal experience with building resilience. I grew up in a middle-class family, with well-educated parents. There was no alcohol or drug use, and to all appearances this was a happy and healthy home. But what went on inside the house was very different from the facade. Both of my parents had been severely wounded in their own lives, were not resilient from their own bruises, and as a result subjected me to significant abuse. I coped by focusing on schoolwork, by relying on friendships, and by escaping into books where good things happened, there was healing in the human condition, and happy endings were possible. I found the resilience to get through a difficult childhood, though it would take much more work—and tapping into my inner core—to fully process, recover, and move on from the experience. Much excavation was necessary for me to rediscover my strengths and goodness.

Everyone possesses resilience, and everyone needs it. Social media can convince us that everybody around us is doing just wonderfully, with no challenges, no crises, and the full support of their spouse and families. We wonder: *Why me? Why do I have these difficulties in my life when others don't?* But we never really know what's going on in someone else's life. The reality is that we all have challenges and we all have hardships. We all need resilience.

I offer this book as a practical and supportive guide to help you connect with your everyday resilience and nourish and grow that inner well of strength and proficiency. In each chapter you'll read about real-life individuals—their struggles, their growth, and their victories. And you'll learn practical, easy-to-follow strategies that will enable you to draw on your resilience to cope with challenges big and small.

You'll see a few key themes cropping up throughout the book. The first is the importance of mindfulness, that is, an awareness of what's going on in our minds, and in the here and now. An incredibly useful approach, mindfulness enables us to see what's real and true in our experience, and with that we can determine our next steps with much greater clarity. Second, we'll explore the fact that what we focus on tends to become our reality: If we attend to what's going well and our own strengths, we'll become more likely to see the positive elements in our lives. Along with that comes the understanding that the human brain is highly malleable. Modern neuroscience shows us that our own brains are remapping and growing new connections every moment of our lives. There is truly little about our mind-set that's fixed, and this good news sets the stage for many evidence-based practices that you'll use to cultivate resilience.

Finally, always keep in mind that we have many choice points in our lives. It's true that the challenges and adversities we face can be beyond our control. But resilience is largely about the choices we can make regarding that which *is* under our control. Far from being a passive endurance of life's tribulations, resilience is an active process with which you can choose to engage. As we explore the key factors that cultivate resilience—connection, flexibility, perseverance, self-regulation, positivity, and self-care—you'll gain clarity on the many choice points you have.

My hope is that this book will provide just the right mix of information and practical strategies. As you read, you'll be reclaiming your birthright: your ability to enjoy life and thrive, no matter what difficulty comes your way.

CHAPTER 1

Cultivate Your Resilience

You might think of resilience as something extraordinary—the stuff of heroes and heroines, a strength that goes beyond us mere mortals. But here's the truth: We are all resilient. Resilience is a power that we all carry inside of ourselves.

For many of us, though, our inborn capacity to be resilient is never fostered or nurtured. And so that ability stays dormant because we never learned how to draw from the well of strength that's within us. But it's never too late to change that. Each of us can grow our resilience in a variety of ways, and in this chapter we'll start that process. You'll gain clarity about your deep inner resilience and learn that you can rewire your brain to cultivate this powerful resource.

Becoming More Resilient

What does "resilience" mean to you? When you think of resilience, you may think of a rubber band, bouncing back to normal after being stretched apart. Or perhaps you envision something like a willow tree, bending in a strong gust of wind but not breaking. Those are relevant images, but I see resilience as something more than being able to bend or bounce back. Resilience is a renewable strength that lies within us, upon which we can draw to provide what we need to meet the challenges we face. I offer this definition:

> **Resilience** *is a well of inner resources that allows you to weather the difficulties and challenges you encounter without unnecessary mental, emotional, or physical distress.*

Your Inner Well of Resilience

More than just rebounding after a setback, resilience is about inner strength, resources, wisdom, and goodness. Our inner well of resilience contains whatever we need to fortify our hearts and minds so we can navigate the difficulties we face. It's always with us, to help us move from feeling overwhelmed to knowing that we can handle things. Challenges will always arise; they're an inescapable part of life. When you draw from your resilience, however, you have the tools you need to face these challenges, and to do so without going under. Your well of resilience helps you meet adversity, large or small, and overcome whatever obstacles are in your path.

Imagine now, as you're reading these words, that you're standing in front of such a well. And it's filled with cool, clear, sparkling fresh water: water that nourishes and sustains, helping all living things grow.

Take a moment to imagine drinking from this well; imagine what this feels like. Do you feel a sense of relaxation in your body? Do you feel calmer? In this book, you'll learn how to draw from this well to meet whatever difficulty you encounter.

Let's look at two people who accessed their wells of resilience in the face of challenges. (All the names used in this book have been changed to protect the privacy of those involved.)

> Jennifer was a 44-year-old mother of two and first grade teacher whose life took a dramatic turn when she was diagnosed with multiple sclerosis. Previously an avid runner, as her condition progressed, she required two canes to walk, and the future course of her illness was uncertain. Jennifer felt overwhelmed by loss and was unsure how she'd manage. She considered giving up teaching but realized that her students brought much joy and meaning to her life. She found that no matter what had been taken from her, remaining in the classroom helped give her strength to keep moving forward. The challenges were many, yet this sense of meaning helped her cope with everything that arose.

> Jeffrey was a 27-year-old engineer who'd struggled with anxiety on and off since his teens. His mind was often occupied with worries about how others perceived his words and actions. He often awoke during the night replaying conversations in which he thought he'd come up short. His fingernails were chewed to the quick, and he wondered if he was getting an ulcer. After his girlfriend of many years told him she'd found someone else, he entered therapy. He also attended a mindfulness course and found that staying in the present and questioning his thoughts helped dampen the anxiety and sadness he'd been feeling. Soon he found that meditation and yoga replenished his sense of balance within, steadying him in periods of darkness.

Why is it that some people grow stronger from adversity, while others develop stress-related conditions like post-traumatic stress disorder or depression? Why do some become pessimistic, demoralized, cynical, and angry, while others move forward with renewed optimism and compassion? Why do some people seem to ride the waves of day-to-day difficulty and come out ahead, while others are paralyzed making even minor decisions? Modern science provides some answers, though it also leaves many questions. We know that a complex interplay of biological, psychological, social, spiritual, family, and genetic factors influences our response to stress. We also know that there's a unique combination of these in every individual, and that we have more influence over those factors than we may realize.

Finding the Strength Within

Based on my work with thousands of individuals, from hospice patients to trauma survivors to physicians, I've learned that resilience is a fundamental quality within all of us, regardless of the particular set of biological and environmental factors that impact us. We are all born with our own well of resilience, but not everyone learns how to replenish that supply of inner strength after hard times deplete it. Some of us aren't taught that we can grow a core of inner strength and self-love to use to buffer ourselves during times of duress and challenge. We didn't learn that respecting the wisdom we've gained from our experiences helps us be resilient. Nor did we learn that, with resilience, we can be the author of our lives, writing a new ending regardless of what's come before.

Yet these are things that anyone can learn. This book will provide you with the tools to understand and grow your resilience, starting with this chapter's look at the growing science that shows we can train our brains to respond more positively to stress and adversity. Then we'll examine the key components of resilience and how to strengthen each of them in turn. In chapter 2, you'll gain an understanding of how social connections and community fuel resilience, and learn how to grow strong and sustaining relationships. Chapter 3 will explore practical ways to build your mental flexibility so you can see new ways of approaching change and uncertainty. In chapter 4, you'll learn about perseverance and how the science of motivation can help you make shifts in your life. Chapter 5 offers advice for self-regulating the often-fierce emotions that arise in our lives, and the common negative feelings that make it difficult for us to skillfully access our well of resilience. In chapter 6, we'll dive into positive emotions and examine how they fuel growth, health, and creativity. Self-care is our focus in chapter 7, and in chapter 8, you'll review what you learned and make plans to maintain and grow your resilience for the long term.

Along the way, you'll hear more real-life stories of people whose resilience was challenged in large or small ways and how they responded. And throughout, you'll learn specific resilience exercises that will teach you how to put concepts from this book into practice in your everyday life.

Your Chronicle of Resilience

Many of the exercises in this book involve writing as a form of personal reflection. I encourage you to designate a journal to use for the writing exercises and to record any other ideas, notes, or insights on your path to greater resilience. Having everything together will make it easier to track your progress, revisit previous reflections, and review what you've learned.

You Can Rewire Your Brain

When we talk about building our resilience, we're really talking about strengthening the brain's most effective ways of managing stress and responding to threats. Whatever imperfect coping habits you may have, don't worry. Modern science—especially the developing field of neuro-plasticity, or the brain's capacity to reorganize itself—tells us that the human brain has an amazing ability to change its ways. All you need are the right tools to harness your brain's learning power. Let's explore how that works by looking at what our nervous system does behind the scenes when we're exposed to stress.

Fight/Flight/Freeze

Our brain and body have a complex and ingenious system for reacting to threat and danger, known as the *fight/flight/freeze response*. To put it very simply, it operates like this: When there's a stressful stimulus, your sensory system—your eyes, ears, nose, mouth, and skin—sends signals to a part of the brain known as the *amygdala* (sometimes called the fear and alarm center). That part of the brain in turn activates your *sympathetic nervous system*. That's the network of nerves that focus on reacting to danger, triggering physiological responses all over the body that enable us to fight, flee, or freeze until danger has passed. This quick activation was an incredibly useful response for our prehistoric ances-tors. It kept them safe, providing the brief period of intense focus and strength needed to fight a rival band of Neanderthals, sprint away from a saber-toothed tiger, or hunt a woolly mammoth.

Though this system was vital to the survival of our forebears, in current times it often causes more harm than good. Our brains aren't great at distinguishing between a physical threat and a psychological one. And in modern days, our fight/flight/freeze response can be set off by relatively trivial events rather than life-or-death concerns. Social threats (difficulties in relationships, workplace conflicts, stressful family dynamics), worries about the future (*Will I have enough money?*), and even ruminations about past sources of psychological discomfort

(*Why did I say what I said?*) can send our sympathetic nervous system into overdrive.

Even if we intellectually understand that these triggers are trivial, when the rubber hits the road, our instincts can make it difficult to tell the difference between real and imagined threats. A text from a hostile boss, a horn honking at us while we're waiting for a frail elder to cross the road, a reminder of a past traumatic event: All can trigger the fight/flight/freeze survival instinct, setting our sympathetic nervous system into action. Over time, anxiety can become linked with situations, thoughts, and memories that are unrelated to genuine sources of danger—the crash of a dropped water glass sets you on edge because you were recently in a car accident, for example. In this sense, the brain may inadvertently create its own fears.

What happens next is where resilience comes into play. A perceived threat not only triggers the fight/flight/freeze response, but also activates an area of the brain known as the *prefrontal cortex* (PFC). Literally the front part of your brain, this area is in some ways the overseer of all behavior. It's involved in complex thought, expression of personality, decision-making, and moderating social behavior; in other words, it handles a lot of what makes us who we are and keeps us from acting in the interest of short-term rather than long-term goals.

Our survival instinct reacts first in a dangerous situation. This is why we can act without thinking when there's danger—we run from a burning building; we don't first ponder what may have started the fire. But soon after the initial fight/flight/freeze response is activated, the PFC engages and we can take a step back and determine if we're safe from harm or if we were even truly threatened in the first place. The more resilient we are, the easier it is for us to think carefully when something trips our survival alarm.

It's important to monitor our response to stress and be sure that our sympathetic nervous system isn't overreacting. For one thing, we may not act rationally in the face of stress if we don't calm down (returning to the burning building example, you don't want to escape the fire but then run straight into traffic). Second, our fight/flight/freeze response comes with the release of cortisol, a stress hormone that helps the body divert its resources to deal with an immediate source of danger. In the short term, that's fine—our rapid breathing and heart rate bring blood and oxygen to our muscles so we can fight or escape a threat. But if we're frequently stressed and almost constantly producing cortisol, the hormone can wreak havoc on our mental and physical well-being. Anxiety, depression, insomnia, lack of energy, and difficulty concentrating are just a few symptoms of long-term exposure to cortisol.

To summarize: Our brain's fight/flight/freeze instinct can be triggered by all sorts of things in the modern world that aren't actually threats. And reacting in that way is bad for us in the long run. So what's the answer?

All we have to do is rewire our brains.

The Freeze Response

Most of us understand the idea of "fight or flight," but considering the brain's reaction to threats is incomplete without discussion of the freeze response. An instinct to "freeze" or remain immobile kicks in when the brain assesses that there's a danger that can't be fought or escaped. During an overwhelming physical or psychological event that we're unable to escape, this response can cause what's called *dissociation*, a numbing or blurring of our senses and memory. Childhood abuse survivors, for example, may find their memories of the trauma repressed, or stored away until they have the resources needed to cope with them.

Our Malleable Brain

Until about two decades ago, scientists believed that after adolescence the human brain did not change very much. We now understand that the exact opposite is true: Brain structure and function are highly malleable and are almost constantly changing throughout our lives. This is called *neuroplasticity,* the ability of the brain to change and adapt as a result of thoughts, actions, and experiences. And it's fantastic news for building our resilience; in fact, it forms the basis for many of the strategies you're going to learn in this book.

In addition, our brains are very good at recognizing patterns. Take, for example, our ability to make sense of the letters of the alphabet. In truth, letters are simply collections of lines and curves, but our brains have learned that these patterns mean something important. It's groups of strongly connected neurons that are the basis of learning or habit formation, and neuroscientific discoveries are helping us understand that our thoughts, feelings, and physical sensations shape and reshape our neural networks. These networks are almost continuously being "rewired" based on our experiences, and repetitive firing along the same neural pathways within the brain further creates stronger connections and organization of neurons—thus the concept that "neurons that fire together, wire together." This theme is critically important for resilience.

Over time, as repeated activity deepens and strengthens the connections of particular neural networks, they become a kind of mental pathway, a track for your thoughts and behaviors to follow. Repeated thoughts and behaviors deepen the tracks, which is why it can be hard to change your habits. But learning something new, and practicing and repeating it, can create new tracks for your brain's thought processes to follow.

The beauty of this is that what you practice can truly become your reality. If you dwell on your positive experiences, strengths, and successes, your brain becomes more inclined to focus on these qualities as those neural connections grow and deepen. If, on the other hand, you hold on to grudges and resentments, regularly accuse yourself of not being smart enough, and engage in other forms of negative thinking, you'll cultivate your ability to be negative.

It's not that seeing the glass half full makes you happier, it's that savoring positives over and over again builds neural pathways that allow you to see more positives. Meanwhile, the pathways that get less use—those involving worry, fear, and anxiety—diminish. Modern neuroscience points to the importance of intentionally focusing on what is truly going well.

Let's examine this in action.

> John remembered his father as critical and demanding. Often comparing John to his older brother, his father frequently told him that he wasn't smart enough in school or good enough in sports. By adulthood, John had a sense of inadequacy that carried into every aspect of his life. Even the slightest negative feedback activated a sense of fear and anxiety and intense self-scrutiny about how he'd spoken and acted. In his 40s, after yet another love relationship fell apart, John began cognitive behavioral therapy, which focuses on the thoughts, images, beliefs, and attitudes that can lock us into ineffective ways of behaving and dealing with emotional problems. John learned that his own thought patterns were reinforcing his father's mean-spirited and incorrect messages. He began to practice countering these with compassionate and affirming ones, like "I have many strengths. I am a smart and talented person." It took time and effort, but gradually his anxiety lessened and he maintained a more positive, and more accurate, sense of himself.

What John did was develop new neural pathways to replace the ones fostered in his difficult childhood. Though our lives include difficulties that we can't avoid, we can harness the powerful regenerative abilities of our brains to form new connections, and in doing so reshape our reality. John couldn't change the past, but by focusing on the positive, he changed his experience of the present.

A Personal Journey

Developing resilience is a personal process. Each of us reacts differently to the stresses in our lives; your way of coping with a challenging situation could be completely different from someone else's. There's no single right way to manage a challenge and no one-size-fits-all response that will determine the outcome. What's important is that you develop the tools that allow you to face whatever challenges appear on your path in the way that works best for you.

We must each find the formula for resilience that works best for our unique life circumstances. As you move forward in your pursuit of everyday resilience, be cautious of how you evaluate your progress. Most of us excel at judging ourselves harshly, but being generous and compassionate toward yourself is one of the key foundations of resilience. Becoming your own friend and ally is vital, and we will explore this process in chapter 7. Equally important is realizing that wherever you are in your journey right now is exactly where you need to be. In the words of psychologist Carl Rogers, "The curious paradox is that when I accept myself just as I am, then I change."

Your judgments about yourself play a big role in your ability to be resilient. Let's compare how a different point of view in similar circumstances can lead to different outcomes.

Rose was 18 when she developed her first bout of depression. An anxious teen, she was a straight-A student who pushed herself hard. She was also an avid soccer player. She took great pride in all her abilities and was thrilled when she was accepted to her top choice for undergraduate studies in education. In her first semester, however, she struggled socially, not finding a friend group that worked for her, and became more and more isolated. She told herself that she didn't have the right social skills to be as popular as others and blamed herself for the sense of depression she was feeling. She withdrew from social life and spiraled down. Engulfed in despair, she stopped attending classes, then dropped out and moved back in with her parents.

Alissa was also 18 when depression hit. Like Rose, Alissa was a star student and had talents in sports and the arts. Accepted at the school of her choice, her freshman year began as a time of excitement and exploration. By the second semester, however, she started slipping. She had problems concentrating on her class work, was sleeping poorly, and found it difficult to be around others. She reminded herself that depression is an illness, connected with a campus counselor, and pushed herself to stay engaged with her roommate and others. It wasn't an easy time, but she was able to regain her footing. By the end of the school year, she'd rebounded and was back on track.

What explains the differences between these two young women? It's clear that they each had a different explanatory style; in other words, they explained events to themselves in different ways, particularly with relation to their own behavior. The way we perceive, process, and attach meaning to events is typically more critical than the nature of the actual event, especially in the case of depression and anxiety.

Although both women were externally similar, Rose could be very hard on herself. Sadly, as her depression worsened, she increasingly blamed herself. Alissa, on the other hand, asserted to herself that depression is an illness. This understanding propelled her to seek help early on.

Though all of us are born with tremendous resilience potential, it's often eroded by what each of us faces through the course of our lives. Some of this is societal conditioning: expectations based on gender, race, socioeconomic status, and more that bring pressure and stress into our lives. Regardless of whether we conform to societal norms, it's what occurs in our family and the generational impact of stress, prejudice, poverty, trauma, and violence that all combine to determine how we respond to adversity. And yet, studies suggest that there are innumerable paths to acquiring resilience. While not definitive, research on twins reveals that genetic factors may contribute to approximately **30** percent of a person's resilience. This means that much of resilience comes from both how we're raised and how we relate to the challenges we face—the latter demonstrated by Rose and Alissa's stories. External conditions such as faith and spirituality, family, community support, self-reflection, affinity groups, counseling, and mindfulness practices can also be key components of a person's resilience journey. My goal is to introduce you to a wide range of tools and strategies that you can adapt to fit your own needs.

How This Book Will Help

You're reading this book for a reason. Perhaps you need help navigating a current stressful life event or want to put something you've experienced in perspective. Or maybe you're seeking greater peace, confidence, and balance. Perhaps you want to strengthen key relationships. Maybe you've been struggling with depression, anxiety disorder, or post-traumatic stress disorder. (See your doctor if you suspect you suffer from a serious condition.)

A key part of this process is honoring the story of your life. We all walk the path that life presents us, and we each walk it in a unique way. Circumstances shape who we are, and they're not to be taken lightly. We are all the products of countless influences—some are under our control, while others are not. This book will help you focus on the aspects of your life that *are* in your control, aligning them in the direction of your well-being. You'll become more aware of the many choice points you have in your life and notice you have far more than is often apparent. Seeing the options available to you is a key strategy for strengthening your resilience.

Wherever you are on your path, I'd like to help you fill your well. My life's work has been devoted to providing people with what they need in times of duress and darkness. From my own journey, I know what a difference resilience can make, and I want to help you develop yours.

Here are some points to keep in mind as you continue:

Perfection is a myth. When you're reading this book, please be sure to be kind to yourself. Absorb whatever information is right for you, and don't pressure yourself to take in anything that doesn't fit. Know that you don't have to do everything perfectly to achieve resilience; in fact, there's no such thing as "perfect."

Remember why you're doing this. Like many, you may have a lot going on in your life. Consider this book as an opportunity to take time out of your busyness, to step back and reflect, and to retreat from the stress and worries of the day. If you're struggling to take time away from other commitments, think of building your resilience as an investment in yourself and your life. A chance to reflect on your own journey, the information in this book will get you thinking about questions such as:

> What kind of events have been most difficult for me?
>
> Where have I found the support I've needed?
>
> How have the challenges in my path shaped who I am today?
>
> What have I learned about myself that I can apply to my current difficulties?

Exploring questions such as these will help you discover what you need to deepen and maintain your inner well of resilience. Putting some activities on hold for now will mean you'll be better able to attend to them later.

This is a process. Just like building muscles at the gym, strengthening your resilience is an ongoing project that yields increasing benefits over time. Don't expect to become suddenly resilient overnight with one reading of this or any other book. You'll find a variety of resilience exercises in these pages that you can keep using as your resilience grows. And developing resilience is not a one-size-fits-all plan: I've included many types of practices, knowing that we all learn in our own unique way.

You can plan your own path. Building resilience is often a non-linear experience. I myself have had periods of growth and healing, and equal periods of tremendous pain and difficulty. Highs, lows, and everything in between . . . you probably have them, too. I hope you'll read this book from cover to cover, but I encourage you to open to whatever page speaks to you if that's what you prefer. You'll be sure to find a tidbit that you can mull over or discuss with a friend, and hopefully it will become a starting point for your particular voyage.

Wherever you are on your journey, I want you to know that there's always hope. I'm not just saying that as a platitude; I've seen it again and again in my own life and with the patients and clients with whom I've worked. There is always a way to move toward the things that matter in your life and feed your well-being. There's always sustenance available from the well of resilience inside you, even when it feels most depleted. No matter how dark the time in your life, that well is never as empty as it seems, and you always have the ability to replenish it.

KEY TAKEAWAYS

- Resilience is a well of inner resources that allows you to weather the difficulties and challenges you encounter. Each of us has resilience inside us, a deep well that we can draw from and replenish.

- Our brain's alarm system can be overactive, so that minor upsets trigger our primitive fight/flight/freeze response, which causes distress and, over time, produces anxiety and a myriad of physical symptoms.

- Our brains are highly malleable and almost constantly changing.

- With intention and practice, we can change our mental pathways, replacing self-criticism and other negative tendencies with more resourceful, healthy patterns of thought and behavior.

- What resilience looks like is different for each one of us. It's truly a personal journey.

- Most of our resilience is due to environmental factors. Faith, family, community support, self-reflection, affinity groups, counseling, mindfulness, and other elements can be key components of a person's unique resilience journey.

- Self-compassion and avoiding self-judgment are key for building resilience.

CHAPTER 2

Connection

Connection to others is at the heart of resilience. Without connection, our well of resilience dries up and our well-being is at serious risk. In fact, loneliness is as powerful a risk factor for cardiac disease and stroke as a sedentary lifestyle. For many, our family bonds, especially with our parents, are our first source of connection. But even if we don't receive a good dose of parental love and affection, we can establish important bonds with other people throughout our lives, in many different ways. From small moments of resonance shared with strangers to building relationships with friends and partners, from volunteer work that connects us to our community to performing random acts of kindness, every connection we make builds our resilience.

Cultivate Connection

We human beings are social creatures, so it should come as no surprise that resilience and psychological health in general are inextricably linked to our ability to connect with others., Our ancestors' survival depended on banding with others for mutual support in a harsh, dangerous world; lack of connection could truly lead to death. From an evolutionary standpoint, social affiliation is hardwired into our species, and our emotional health is sustained by our bonds with other people.

Our need for social connection begins when we're born and has an ongoing impact on our lives. In a study conducted by researchers at Duke University that tracked the growth of over 400 babies into adulthood, data showed that infants with affectionate and attentive mothers grew up to be happier, less anxious, and more adaptable adults. Conversely, children without parental love and affection displayed less resilience, lower self-esteem, and more aggressive behavior later in life.

But what if we're not fortunate in the hand we're dealt vis-à-vis our biological family? What if our parents or siblings were harsh, withdrawn, or downright abusive? Here, connection with others is even more important. For myself, my relationship with a trusted therapist wove the fabric of connection that was integral to my healing and growth.

The journey life takes each of us on is often bumpy. Our social connections foster the necessary security for our self-regulation (which we'll discuss in chapter 5) and confidence, strengthening our ability to withstand whatever challenges and setbacks we encounter.

Let's look at a real-life example.

> The youngest of three boys, Rob was 10 when he decided he wanted to become a physician. His father abandoned the family shortly after Rob's birth, and his alcoholic mother struggled to hold down a job. There was little stability in his home life. Rob was smart and industrious, however, and did well in school. But he was unsure of himself and didn't have role models for life success. In third grade, a

teacher came into Rob's life who saw Rob's potential and believed in him in a way others had not. Rob's confidence grew as his teacher challenged him with more difficult math problems and reading assignments, and his teacher became a role model and a profound source of validation. Looking back, Rob credits that relationship with a sense that someone was there for him, providing the assurance and security that helped him see that he could use his academic talents to pave a path different from the one into which he'd been born.

Filling our well with connection and support spurs upward spirals, broadening and building our cognitive, psychological, and physical flexibility and resourcefulness, and helping us view challenges and failures as opportunities to grow and learn. Positive relationships foster happiness, love, and confidence in the face of obstacles, which in turn cultivates the resilience that promotes further positive relationships.

The alternative to human connection is grim: Loneliness and social isolation have been linked to high blood pressure, weakening of the immune system, and increased risk of cardiac disease and stroke. In fact, physicians now consider loneliness one of the six major cardiac risk factors—as dangerous as smoking and inactivity. Yet with the time we spend online and on our devices growing, and the time we spend face-to-face shrinking, we're witnessing an epidemic of loneliness. Texting and social media fit with the expediency we've grown to expect in the digital age, but it's direct human contact that really fills our well of resilience.

Just as plants require sunlight and water, humans require love and connection. Romantic love may come to mind when we talk about connecting with other people, but what we're talking about here is what psychology researcher Barbara Fredrickson describes as moments of warmth and connection that we share with another living being, even our pets. In fascinating research studies, she's helped us understand that casual interactions can have moments of resonance, times when we experience a sense of connection, warmth, and positive emotion. These often-tiny moments are like engines that drive the positive upward spiral of resilience. When they occur, they trigger our brain to release *oxytocin*, the same chemical released in moments of heart-throbbing romantic love. Often dubbed the "love" or "cuddle" hormone, oxytocin dampens fear, increases trust, and builds calm.

In her book *Love 2.0*, Fredrickson shines a light on the many instances of this kind of love and connection that we may experience in our everyday lives. Laughter with a friend, the kind smile of a passing stranger on our way to work, interacting with our barista, petting a cat or dog . . . Connection is so important to the human experience that these brief moments have an outsize effect on us. We don't realize it, but these micro-moments of connection bolster our resilience by magnifying trust, increasing our ability to manage our emotions, and even making up for past neglect. And when we pay more attention to these small but meaningful experiences, we get more out of them, almost doing double duty in filling our well of resilience.

Alongside these micro-moments, deeper relationships that nourish our resilience can come in many forms. These include ties with our biological family, but close friendships can be just as important. In fact, a meaningful connection can be formed with anyone, be they friends, coworkers, or fellow members of faith communities, special interest groups, or online forums.

Nor does someone need to be a lifelong friend to bring the benefits of connection. Emotional support can be derived from more recently developed social relationships as well as long-standing ones. Quality trumps quantity here. Having one or two relationships in which we're acknowledged and can speak openly about what's important to us is typically more nourishing than having multiple superficial acquaintances.

Whether they're with a friend or a sibling, a new acquaintance or an old buddy, it's the strongest relationships in our lives that most nurture our resilience. It's important to keep these connections healthy by managing the challenges that naturally arise in any relationship. Here's an exercise that will help you safeguard the relationships on which your resilience depends.

RESILIENCE PRACTICE: Relationship Repair

Cultivating positive connections takes work. We can all veer off course and become focused on what's not going well within a relationship, as opposed to noticing what's working. Yet with practice, we can learn and grow from the struggles our relationships bring, building our empathy for others and growing our resilience to meet further challenges. When the bond you have with someone important to you experiences strain, this practice will help you keep the connection from fraying.

1. Take 15 minutes to sit quietly and think about a conflict you're experiencing with someone who is important to you. Reflect on the situation. Is it something the other person said? Something they did or didn't do? Take note of the emotions you're experiencing as you consider the circumstances.

2. In your journal or notebook, answer each of these questions. Take your time and write as much or as little as feels appropriate.

   - What's important to me about this relationship?
   - How might this challenge we're having look through their eyes?
   - What do I appreciate about this person?
   - What do we both stand to gain by working through this conflict?

3. When you're finished writing, review these questions and reflect on the answers.

   - What did this exercise help you see?
   - Did you notice any change in your emotions?
   - Did adopting the perspective of the other person open any options for resolving the conflict?

CONTINUED

Often, taking time to reflect can help us realize that the conflict isn't as big as it seems, and restore our awareness of what's deeply important to us. Even if this exercise didn't solve the conflict, hopefully it helped you put the issue in the broader context of what's important to you about this person and your relationship with them. The next time you have a conflict, try to find time to conduct this exercise before you decide how to resolve the disagreement.

Being able to navigate the challenges that arise in relationships is a core life skill. By taking this time to reflect, you're strengthening your ability to learn from whatever challenges come your way. In other words, you're growing your resilience.

The Power of Relationships

We've seen that building and maintaining positive relationships brings a remarkable host of benefits. Social connection can bolster your resilience by building trust, providing positive role models, and fostering encouragement and reassurance. Let's examine each of these more closely.

Trust

The adversities we face in life can be so intense that they rob us of a sense of trust in the world and in people. We find it hard to believe that the world can be a safe place, or that we can depend on anyone. So caught up in what we can't trust, we may lose sight of what we can. We can even lose our ability to trust connection itself. But while we may long to retreat and go inward, rebuilding this trust through love and connection is a path to greater resilience. As a highly connected species, we need others to lean on, to validate us, and to affirm our worthiness.

Sometimes when we go through hard times, we can feel that life has not been fair to us. It's easy to imagine a plan of how our life should be, a storybook concept that's reinforced by movies and books. We can find ourselves using this as a guidepost and feel cheated because things aren't going the way we think they're supposed to. But our social connections remind us that everybody suffers and that bumps in the road are just the way life is. Our suspicion of being treated unfairly is replaced by a trust that we're all actually in the same boat.

Role Models

Our parents or caregivers are our first and primary role models; they're the ones we spend the most time with as children, observing their behavior and imitating what we see. If our parents show affection, we know we are loved; we feel a solid sense of connection and we develop a sense of our worth. If they model calmness, attentiveness, and empathy, we trust that we can be seen and heard. If they see our strengths and efforts, we learn to see these as well. In a sense, good parenting involves holding up a mirror to a child's strengths and goodness. This enables children to develop those strengths, resilience included.

Whether or not our primary caregivers were models of healthy, positive behavior, others throughout our lives can become examples that we follow. Consider individuals who you've seen conquer major life challenges: family members, friends, or people you've read about. A role model isn't always the person you'd expect. Interestingly, when I ask physicians whom they hold up as their role models for resilience, the answer is almost always a patient who faced their illness with grace. Additionally, it's typically a patient who's moved from trying to meet the expectations of others toward focusing on what's truly important for them.

Reflect for a moment on someone you strongly admire, someone either living or deceased: a family member, a spiritual figure, a political or historic figure, or perhaps even a fictional character from a book or movie. What is it that you admire about them? Are these qualities you'd like to emulate? Thinking about this person's attributes can help you identify the resilience features that are most meaningful for you.

Encouragement and Reassurance

A young child goes on a swing alone for the first time, looking to a parent for validation and reassurance. You finish an assignment that you've worked hard on; your boss sees your efforts and voices approval. Verbally and nonverbally, the encouragement, validation, and reassurance we get from others is pivotal for our well-being. These moments of affirmation are another example of the micro-moments of positivity we mentioned earlier, almost as important as experiencing warmth or love. In childhood, these moments build our self-confidence. Whether or not our childhood was full of such moments, as adults we can embrace them when they occur.

As a coach, I see over and over again how important a supportive, validating, and non-judgmental space can be. Having someone believe that we're naturally creative, resourceful, and whole fosters our ability to develop resourcefulness and manage whatever challenge we're facing. Encouragement that we receive through a supportive helping presence, even in brief moments, empowers us to handle adversity and adds to our well of resilience.

RESILIENCE PRACTICE:
Embracing Micro-Moments of Connection

Whether you're young or older, single or married, an introvert or extrovert, it's normal to sometimes experience loneliness. Often we try to manage loneliness by engaging in texting, emails, or social media, but these impersonal forms of communication may not provide the connection that a real-time or in-person interaction can. Instead, take advantage of the micro-moments that bring you brief but meaningful connections with others. Many of these are already going on in your life, and this exercise will help you take notice of these moments, amplifying the burst of oxytocin and other positive effects that they bring. Writing about them adds to the benefit even more.

Starting today, spend one week trying to tune in to three micro-moments of connection daily, following these guidelines:

Pay attention to your interactions. Try to be fully present when you have small encounters with strangers, acquaintances, and everyone you meet. Focus on what you experience in these moments of connection. Notice how your body feels.

Encourage connection. At work and at home, look at the facial expression of the other person and take in what you see. Push yourself to smile at the people you interact with.

Keep a log. At the end of every day, describe three moments of connection in your journal. For each, apply the following statements and score them on a scale of 0 (not true at all) to 5 (absolutely true).

During the interactions:

I felt "in tune" with the other person.

I felt a sense of closeness to the other person.

I noticed a sense of warmth in my body.

My body relaxed.

My problems seemed smaller.

Notice whether consciously looking for micro-moments of connection also deepens your important relationships, sensitizing you to the feelings of connection they bring. See if the exercise enhances your overall mood. Perhaps

CONTINUED

you feel more generous with others, for example. Record these thoughts in your journal, too.

You don't have to keep logging your micro-moments, but do try to make it a habit to notice and value them. Micro-moments of connection nourish your mind, body, heart, and soul. The more you can take in these moments, the more you're filling your well of resilience, gaining ballast to weather whatever storms come your way.

Service to Others

In the competitive society we live in, it's easy to focus on what's in it for us, rather than what's in it for others. An overly self-focused reality, centered on I, me, and mine, however, contributes to disconnection and loneliness. And paradoxically, all this focus on ourselves makes us more vulnerable because it depletes our well of resilience. To paraphrase the Dalai Lama: "Thinking mainly of ourselves contributes to unhappiness. Thinking of others is a recipe for happiness." As mentioned earlier, when we're lacking social connection, we start thinking that we're the only one suffering, that others have it easier than us, or that life is unfair. Helping others grounds us in the truth that suffering is part of being human. One way or another, we all face obstacles and challenges.

The popular book and movie *Pay It Forward* illustrate how acts of kindness and generosity are like ripples in a pond, their impact radiating outward in both expected and unexpected ways. Just as Rob's teacher (page 20) gave Rob vital support and encouragement, helping others is a way we can pay forward the support that we ourselves have received. In return, we gain just as much as those we help. Numerous studies reveal that altruism and volunteering correlate positively with increased life satisfaction, decreased depression, lower blood pressure, and even increased longevity.

That's an especially important truth these days. With the increasing role of technology in our lives and digitalization of our world, our day-to-day interactions seem to be losing human elements and cues like facial expression and voice tone. In her book *The Empathy Effect*, my Harvard Medical School colleague Helen Riess, MD, explains that this is why we see so much vitriol and outright bullying in the digital space. Helping others can be an antidote to these societal trends that favor individuation, self-gain, and dog-eat-dog patterns. When we serve others, we're reminded that other people are full human beings just as we are. This feeling of connectedness strengthens our resilience and counteracts feelings of isolation.

> Loretta had always wanted to have children. But after chemotherapy for Hodgkin's lymphoma in her early 30s, she found out that she was infertile. She and her husband considered adoption, something Loretta wanted, but her husband couldn't imagine bonding with a child who wasn't his biological offspring. Loretta threw herself into her career, and her life was full with the demands of her work. But there was a nagging sense of emptiness that she couldn't quite shake. When a friend mentioned that a local children's hospital was seeking volunteers to hold and rock infants in the neonatal intensive care unit, Loretta signed up without hesitation. The moment she first held one of the newborns, she felt a rush of maternal love and warmth. Soon she was volunteering weekly. Loretta described the experience as bringing a sense of wholeness that she hadn't realized was missing from her life. She knew she was making a difference in these tiny babies' lives, and she was also filling her well of resilience by nourishing a part of her soul.

There are countless ways to help others. Like Loretta, you can volunteer with a local hospital or charitable group. Along with formal volunteering, you can express altruism every day through what's come to be known as *random acts of kindness*. These are selfless acts to help or cheer up someone else, done for no reason other than to make someone happier. We know that our brain is constantly learning and adapting from our experiences, and that what we focus on becomes more deeply established in our psyche, so each act of kindness you perform makes the next one a little easier. And the recipient of your kindness is likely to pass it along: When someone is generous to us, it softens an inner sense of deprivation that can lead us to be stingy with others. Kindness is truly contagious.

RESILIENCE PRACTICE: Acts of Kindness

For some, signing up to do volunteer work on a regular basis fits with their schedule, and a formal commitment keeps them engaged with helping. Another approach is random acts of kindness. These brief, simple actions don't take much effort: feeding a stranger's parking meter, picking up trash in your local park, donating blood, leaving a thank-you note for a coworker, or offering assistance to an elderly neighbor. Helping someone else gives you a small boost of connection and positivity, adding water to your well.

This week, perform at least three acts of kindness for others. You can plan these ahead of time, or simply stay alert for appropriate opportunities. Your kind acts do not all need to be toward the same person, and the beneficiaries can be strangers or people you know. You don't have to act in secret, but the recipient also doesn't need to be aware of your actions; credit isn't the point. Go for variety whenever you can, trying out a novel act as often as possible.

After each act of kindness, write down what you did in your journal. Make a note of how performing this act of kindness felt for you. Notice the emotions that arise and any physical sensations. Take note of your mood before and after you perform the act. Did anything shift?

KEY TAKEAWAYS

- Human beings are hardwired for connection.

- Loneliness is as powerful a risk factor for cardiac disease and stroke as a sedentary lifestyle.

- Romantic relationships aren't the only way to fill our need for connection. Friendships and micro-moments of connection with others can be equally important.

- Our social connections strengthen our resilience because they help us develop trust, provide us with role models, and bring us reassurance and encouragement.

- Service to others benefits the one who gives as well as the one who receives.

- Random acts of kindness are small moments of generosity that build resilience in us and encourage the recipients to pass the kindness along.

CHAPTER 3

Flexibility

As we touched on in chapter 1, resilience is often associated with the concept of flexibility: to bend without breaking, to stretch without being pulled out of shape. Certainly, physical strength and flexibility complement each other very well; Think of the way that athletes or yoga practitioners train their bodies to be both strong and flexible. But the flexibility that comes with resilience is more than an ability to endure tribulations and return to normal. When we're resilient, we have cognitive and emotional flexibility. We have the adaptability to look at things with new eyes and to better evaluate our own circumstances. A key tool for developing this type of flexibility is mindfulness, a practice that we'll examine in more detail in this chapter.

Cultivate Flexibility

We can easily get locked into a certain a way of viewing things—our life, ourselves, and the things that happen to us. Though many of the circumstances of our lives are beyond our ability to change, we can *always* change how we view them. Two people who experience the same event can view them in completely different ways. One of us might ask, "Why does this type of thing keep happening to me?" while the other might see good fortune with the bad, considering it an opportunity to make positive changes.

We tend to forget that our expectations of what will happen next are often completely wrong. A situation that looks like it's going to be terrible can turn out to be just the right thing. Suppose your significant other ends the relationship, and you're devastated. You don't see how you'll ever find someone else. After time, however, you begin online dating and answer an ad for someone whose profile you never would have previously considered. This person becomes the love of your life. If you'd remained locked into the assumption that you had no hope of finding romance again, you never would have discovered that an even better relationship awaited you.

Here's an example where flexible thinking could have made a big difference.

> As he was leaving work the Friday before Thanksgiving, Tom
> was informed that his job was being cut. He was devastated.
> Over that weekend, in addition to worries about money, he
> found himself thinking, *Why is this happening to me? I'm
> such a failure. Everyone knows that I always mess every-
> thing up. Right before Thanksgiving. I have the worst luck
> of anyone.* Absorbed in worry and rumination, Tom slept
> poorly that week and was irritable with his wife and kids.
> When his out-of-town relatives arrived for the holiday, he
> was so distracted and absorbed in his negative thoughts
> that he barely connected with them. The holiday he'd been
> looking forward to for weeks passed by without any enjoy-
> ment or warmth.

We can use Tom's experience to illustrate how we respond to diffi-cult events in our lives. Specifically, the story demonstrates the concept known as the *first and second arrows of pain and suffering.*

The *first arrow* is the event itself. We can't control this arrow. In this case, it was Tom losing his job, something nobody wants to go through. Of course, fear, worry, and anxiety are part of this experience. Life is full of adverse events like job loss, illness, and accidents; the pain from them is unavoidable.

The *second arrow*, however, comes to us through the story that we develop about what happened. We can obsess over self-blame, poor luck, and lack of fairness. The second arrow is where our mind takes the basic facts of the situation and then goes a step further and draws conclusions and makes inferences, often traveling into the past and future to a place of fear, anger, insecurity, worry, anxiety, and even depression.

Often this reaction is based on patterns of thinking established in our early life experiences, those neural pathways that we tread over and over again. As with Tom, the second arrow frequently takes the form of a harsh voice of judgment about ourselves. For Tom, it was bad enough that he'd lost the job, but the second arrow of intense self-judgment made his experience worse and took his mind away from what could have been a restorative holiday with his family.

Understanding this concept can powerfully build the flexibility that promotes our resilience. Consider for a moment any difficulty you're currently facing. Think about the primary problem, the event that's set you back: a strain in an important personal relationship, a health issue, a major work task you're struggling to complete. That's the first arrow, what we might consider to be the facts of the matter.

The second arrow is where your mind goes with these facts. For the strained relationship, your mind might jump to *It's not fair that this person treated me this way,* or *Why does this always happen to me?* For a health issue, it might be a succession of fears that your ailment will make it impossible for you to perform your work or care for your kids. For the work task, it could be anxiety that others won't see the value of your work, or a belief that your performance on this task will make or break a hoped-for raise.

In seeing the second arrow, we can recognize how our minds produce worry and anxiety based on assumptions that may or may not be true. Let's think about some other possible interpretations. What if similar relationship strains are simply a normal part of human connection, neither fair nor unfair? And what if the health issue turns out to be less serious and doesn't impact your abilities? Further, you don't know how people will view your work or whether your boss will put much emphasis on this project. After all, we can never truly know what's going to happen in the future. The point here is that we jump to conclusions— and these conclusions cause us quite a bit of strife.

What are the second arrows for the difficulty you've brought to mind? Can you see how your mind can take you on a painful journey that adds to the difficulty of the primary event? How might you reconsider or address your assumptions of what's to come? On the one hand, you may be spot-on about your concerns, but, on the other, the series of worries may not portend what will actually come to pass. Perhaps you could get help with your work task, or build your confidence by remembering your successes with similar projects. Maybe the person you're upset with didn't intend to hurt you, or was just having a bad day. Stopping to "unpack" the second arrow can help you work with your own mind, decreasing much unnecessary stress.

As the saying goes, "I have been through some terrible things in my life, most of which never happened." In Tom's example, the point is not that Tom was to blame for experiencing the second arrow; we're all prone to that. But recall that our definition of resilience includes avoiding *unnecessary* mental, emotional, and physical distress. Much of the second arrow's effect on us is unnecessary; it's a product of how we react to an event that's upset us. But how do we gain the flexibility to dodge that second arrow, reacting to difficulty in a more positive, flexible way?

The Power of Mindfulness

One way is to learn to use one of the most important tools for building resilience: the practice of *mindfulness*. This increasingly popular approach is often associated with meditation. But in its simplest form, mindfulness means focusing one's attention on the present moment. If we can do this, we can differentiate our mental narrative from the reality of our experience and see that the stories of guilt, shame, or blame that we tell ourselves are actually fiction. With mindfulness, we stop ruminating on the past or writing the future. We come back to the present moment, the one right now, where things usually aren't as bad as our mind may be suggesting.

We can develop mindfulness in a variety of ways, but meditation is the most effective method. When we sit quietly and pay attention to our own thoughts, we learn a lot about just what our mind is up to. It turns out that our minds produce a massive number of thoughts, up to 70,000 a day. Paying attention to them during meditation reveals a few things. First, it shows us that there's a repetitive quality to our thoughts; our minds are quite good at covering the same ground over and over again. Second, we can observe that many of our thoughts are negative judgments: *I don't like that. I'm too fat. This day is going to be awful.* It's almost as if there's a narrator inside our heads, producing a constant stream of commentary about ourselves, our circumstances, and everyone around us. The constant ebb and flow of these thoughts can pull us in all sorts of directions, each taking us away from what's truly unfolding in front of us.

Yet through mindfulness techniques, we can also come to realize that our thoughts are transient, almost like clouds in the sky. They arise, pass through, then fade away. Some may be light and fluffy, while others are downright stormy. The problem is that we often get rigidly attached to our thoughts, and instead of living life and experiencing events for ourselves, we let our minds tell us what our experience is. If we pay attention to what's actually going on, we realize that the narrator in our head often gets things very wrong. But don't take my word for this. Try it and see for yourself.

RESILIENCE PRACTICE: Open Sky Meditation

Here's an easy form of mindfulness meditation that you can practice regularly to improve your awareness of your own thoughts. As you learn to detach from negative thoughts and let them pass, your resilience will increase.

1. Sit comfortably in a quiet space and close your eyes. Bring your attention to your breathing, not trying to control it, just connecting with it. Notice the rise and fall of your chest and feel the air moving in and out of your nose. See if you can keep your focus on this movement, paying attention to how it feels. Try to follow one entire breath from beginning to end, focusing purely on your physical sensations.

2. Now imagine that your mind is like the sky, vast and spacious, without beginning or end. It's a sunny day, and your sky is majestic and bright. When a thought or emotion comes into your mind, take note of it and imagine that it's a cloud in your blue sky, gently passing by. See it arise, move across, and fade away. Easily and naturally, the thought passes through your mind. Just like the sky, your mind is undisturbed by the clouds that inhabit it. It remains open, calm, and expansive.

3. Continue observing your thoughts as if they were clouds in the sky. Just as clouds are a natural part of the sky, so are your thoughts a natural part of you. There's nothing wrong with your mind for producing thoughts, whatever they may be. Without trying to force or control them, let the thoughts pass through gently and without judgment. Simply observe.

4. When you notice that a thought is dominating your attention, try to bring your attention back to your breathing. At certain times this will be easier than

at others. Some thoughts may be like storm clouds; that's okay. Simply notice a difficult or troubling thought and see if you can let it pass by without getting swept away by it. Every time you notice a thought, that's a moment of mindfulness. See if you can commend yourself for paying attention. That's what meditation is all about.

Continue this meditation for at least 10 minutes, then gently open your eyes. Try doing this practice a few times a week, then daily. If you can't fit in 10 minutes, even a few minutes of meditation will help.

Change Is Constant

It's a fundamental law of nature: Everything is impermanent and change is truly the only constant. We experience this truth every day; whether it's with the weather, our bodies, or our thoughts, we're all intimately familiar with the inevitability of change. And yet so much of the difficulty and challenge we experience in our lives stems from not accepting this essential reality. We often think that the way things are is the way they're always going to be, or that we can stop things from changing if we try hard enough. Or we carry some fixed, unchangeable plan in our head, and we're distraught when reality moves in an unanticipated direction.

Being resilient means that we accept the reality of change and in doing so are prepared to bend and adapt with it to avoid unnecessary anguish, pain, and suffering. Unfortunately, many aspects of the culture we live in promote the belief that we can avoid both change and suffering: that we can somehow avoid all illness, or that if we buy the right beauty product, we'll avoid the physical changes of aging. But when we pause and consider this, we see that all humans are vulnerable to change. It's something we all have in common.

We can find resilience in the face of change by considering a different point of view. Buddhist traditions offer an alternative viewpoint that's critically important for developing resilience. Buddhism describes *three marks of existence*, three inescapable qualities of the reality of life.

The **first mark** is that bad things happen and suffering occurs. This is a basic, unavoidable fact. None of us will get through life without experiencing some adversity. For some of us, hardship and misfortune are considerable; for others, they're minor. Most of us are somewhere in between. But for all of us, there is no escaping this first mark. Nevertheless, how often do we find ourselves unable to accept that something's going awry or compare ourselves to someone else, thinking we have it bad while they never have to struggle? Accepting the first mark can spare us this unneeded anguish, affording us more flexibility to roll with the punches life throws at us.

The **second mark** of existence is that everything changes. Nothing is permanent. Our bodies, our relationships, and our environment are always changing. This is also true of our thoughts and emotions. But do we accept this truth gracefully and with ease? Most definitely not! And we're a bit fussy about it to boot. We want the things we like to stay exactly as they are, and we want the things we don't like to transform into something else as soon as possible. But we suffer unnecessarily when we hang on tightly to the ephemeral good things, and when we uselessly rail against the longer-lasting bad things.

Now, the **third mark** of existence might sound odd: There is no self. I encourage you to explore Buddhist teachings further, if you like, to learn the deeper meanings of that statement. For now, like other Western authors, I'm going to simplify here and say that the third mark has to do with how much ego we have. In other words, our minds tend to be constructed with us at the center. We typically see the words and actions of others as being about us. What the third mark helps us see is how little in life is truly about us.

I'll draw on my own experience to illustrate this. I've told you that I grew up in a very abusive home. The abuse involved repeated assaults on my body and left me with a deep sense of shame. As children tend to do, I believed that my father's abuse was my fault, that somehow I was to blame for it. After many years of healing and replenishing my well of resilience, I now know that I never had reason to feel shameful in any way. I was not the cause; I was an innocent and vulnerable child who was, tragically, the target of a very wounded individual's actions.

I share this because it illustrates the far-reaching negative impact that occurs when our mind believes that we are the cause of someone else's actions. Let's look at a less extreme example of the third mark.

Imagine that a coworker sends you a text, asking about your progress on the project you're both working on. You've had some strain with this coworker, and when you read the text you assume that they're accusing you of running behind. You feel attacked, and your fight/flight/freeze instinct is triggered. Before you know it, you're overcome with anxiety, fear, and anger. You fire back with a hostile reply that only serves to fuel the discord. Soon the two of you are swapping angry texts, delaying the project even more and escalating the ill will.

What if your coworker was simply asking for an update, and not accusing? What if their text was less about you and more about their own fears and insecurities about completing the project? Consider times when you've felt hurt, disrespected, or unseen because you took something personally. What would've been different if you had stopped and considered that the incident might not have been personal to you?

Take some time to reflect on the three marks, and you may begin to see how often you suffer because your mind ignores these three basic truths. We all do, of course; our minds are masterful storytellers. But the stories we tell ourselves have the problematic habit of distorting reality. Here's how reminding ourselves of the three marks adds to our well of resilience.

Bad things happen, suffering occurs. If I'm thinking that something difficult shouldn't be happening, I can remember that suffering is part of everyone's lives and is not a deviation from a plan.

Everything changes. If I'm in a difficult spot right now, I can remind myself that this won't always be the case.

I am not at the center. When my teenager tells me I'm the worst parent on the planet for not buying them the latest computer game, I can see that this is not personal. It's simply how teenagers relate to their parents.

RESILIENCE PRACTICE:
Loving-Kindness Meditation

As you build resilience by observing your thoughts and exploring a new viewpoint on pain and suffering, you may feel tempted to judge yourself harshly. *What made me think I'd be immune to suffering? Did I do something wrong by taking something personally? Was I to blame, or was that not my fault at all?* It's a perfectly human tendency to view ourselves and others in a judgmental way. Here's an exercise you can use to replace judgment with compassion, both for yourself and for others.

1. Sit comfortably with your eyes gently closed. Take three slow deep breaths, relaxing areas of tension in your body with each exhalation. Bring your attention inward, giving yourself permission to leave the busyness and worries of your day behind.

2. Bring to mind a person or a pet to whom you feel close. Imagine them standing in front of you. Take in the loving look in their eyes and smile. Mentally recite these words (you can read them off the page until you've committed them to memory):

May you be happy.
May you be healthy in body and mind.
May you be safe from inner and outer danger.
May you live with ease.

3. Now think of a casual acquaintance, someone toward whom you have neither positive nor negative feelings. You and this person are alike in your wish to have resilience and well-being. Mentally recite these words:

Just as I wish to,
May you be happy.
May you be healthy in body and mind.
May you be safe from inner and outer danger.
May you live with ease.

4. Now bring to mind someone with whom you have difficulty. It could be a coworker, neighbor, family member, friend, or anyone else. Even if you feel otherwise, mentally recite these words:

Just as I wish to,
May you be happy.
May you be healthy in body and mind.
May you be safe from inner and outer danger.
May you live with ease.

5. Now imagine sending these same warm wishes to yourself:

May I be happy.
May I be healthy in body and mind.
May I be safe from inner and outer danger.
May I live with ease.

You can even imagine sending these same warm wishes to everyone in your community, or everyone on earth.

CONTINUED

6. Take another three deep breaths. When you're ready, open your eyes. Take a moment to check in with yourself and notice the state of your mind and heart after doing this meditation. Even if this level of compassion seems artificial right now, over time this meditation practice helps us cultivate greater kindness toward ourselves and others.

A Different Point of View

As we noted at the beginning of the chapter, the flexibility of resilience is the openness to seeing things from a new perspective. Accepting that change is the only certainty helps us in a variety of ways. First, it minimizes unnecessary worry, annoyance, frustration, anger, and blame. That's no small thing! When we see that life is what it is, we approach situations and decisions with more flexibility. Think of it like waves on the ocean: If we try to fight the waves—or ignore them—we may very well go under. But if we learn to ride them, we can move with greater agility. Acknowledging the constancy of change can trigger feelings of vulnerability, but it can also provide a secure foundation to rest upon. After all, if we base our faith in something that is fundamentally untrue, we'll be disappointed many times over.

Second, when we accept the reality of change, we shift from a fixed viewpoint into what education researcher Carol Dweck, PhD, calls a *growth mind-set*. With a fixed mind-set, we believe that our abilities are predetermined—that some people are simply better at certain things than others. Though, of course, natural ability varies, that fixed belief can keep us from trying as hard as we might, limiting our sense of possibility. Accepting the reality of change promotes a much more flexible and expansive view, rich with options, including the prospect that we can grow our own talents and learn new skills. We move from a sense of helplessness to one of hope and optimism.

A third perspective shift critical for building resilience is spending less time focusing on what we didn't do well and more time on our positive accomplishments. So often we believe that we're to blame for everything that goes wrong in our lives. Learning from our mistakes is vital, of course. But if we're not careful, we can be so rigidly focused on our faults that we fail to see our strengths and accomplishments. To gain resilience, we have to change our inner critic to an inner ally and move from self-harshness to self-kindness. (We'll discuss how to do that in chapter 7.) When we turn our attention from our flaws to our virtues, we realize that with every challenge we've faced, we've actually applied our strengths to get by. Recognizing those strengths enables us to harness them again to move past current and future obstacles.

Let's look at a story in which a change in perspective eased the initial response to a crisis. Even when our first response to an emergency is one of fear or worry—a perfectly understandable reaction—a shift in perspective afterward can make a big difference.

Roberto was someone who experienced a lot of worry and anxiety in his life. A single dad with two challenging teenagers, he'd recently taken on a new job that he thought would be less stressful, but it turned out that many unexpected duties were added to his plate. When he got the call on a Thursday night that a fire had destroyed his elderly mother's home, he was understandably shocked and fearful. When he and his boys arrived at the scene, he thought his mother looked like she'd aged 10 years.

But once Roberto got her settled into their house, she felt grateful that no one was harmed and they all hugged and laughed together about how stricken she'd looked. Although she'd valued her independence, Roberto and his mother realized that the best solution was for her to stay with him and the boys. Their ability to laugh together, lean into their family ties, and be flexible helped them manage the transition. Spending more time with his mother, watching his children connect with their grandmother, and having her help a bit around the house eased Roberto's anxiety and ended up helping him cope with the demands of his new job.

Roberto's story shows how shifting perspective and viewing a calamity simply as a change to be adapted to can help us recover and open our eyes to new possibilities.

Another benefit of flexibility is realizing that we're not alone in walking a difficult road. It can often appear that other people don't have the problems we have and that somehow life has dealt us a bad hand of cards. But as the first mark reminds us, everyone struggles. Roberto's story shows how an unexpected struggle can sometimes lead to silver linings—in this case helping someone in their time of need—and spending time with those important to us can lighten our own load. We grow our resilience when we accept that life is what it is, forgiving ourselves and others, letting go, and opening ourselves to new approaches.

It takes tremendous courage to look at our lives this deeply and realize that we have the power to reshape our view. Yet each of us has courage deep in our inner well and it's always there for us to draw upon.

RESILIENCE PRACTICE: Your Flexible Toolbox

So often we focus on ways we think we could have acted differently or done better. We regularly berate ourselves and overlook the ways in which we persevered. In this practice, you'll be pushed to look at what you did well, creating more flexibility in how you see your actions during past episodes of adversity.

1. Set yourself in a quiet, comfortable place where you won't be interrupted. This is a writing exercise, so have your journal or other writing material with you.

2. Bring to mind a significant difficulty you've experienced in the past. This could be an illness, the loss of an important relationship or job, an accident, family caregiving responsibilities, or anything else that comes to mind. As you think about this past circumstance, consider the following questions and write the answers in your journal.

   - What resources did you draw upon to overcome the difficulty?
   - What people did you enlist to help and support you?
   - Which of these strengths did you utilize?

     Love of learning

     Patience

     Determination

     Ability to solve problems

     Creativity

     Sense of humor

     Leadership

     Connectedness to others

     Empathy

     Courage

     Other

CONTINUED

Looking back at this experience, answer these questions:

What are you grateful for?

Is there anything you can forgive yourself for?

What are the biggest lessons for you?

3. Based on the strengths you listed, write a paragraph about the experience from a different perspective. Describe how your strengths impacted the outcome, enabling you to overcome the difficulty or getting you through it sooner than you otherwise would have.

Now think about the strengths you exercised in the difficulty you wrote about. How can you apply these to a challenge you are currently experiencing?

By retelling the story of this difficulty from a new perspective, you are replenishing your resilience well by seeing the strength and resourcefulness that you already possess. In doing so, you can get closer to the truth of your experience and build more confidence and steadiness, giving yourself the sure footing that's needed to manage whatever is next.

KEY TAKEAWAYS

- Pain and suffering come in the form of two arrows. Though we can't control the first arrow, we can exert a substantial degree of control over the second.

- Mindfulness allows us to see that our thoughts are transient and that our minds form stories about our existence that are not always true.

- With meditation, we grow our ability to observe our thoughts without judgment and detach from them so they don't sweep us away.

- The three marks of existence remind us that suffering is part of life, that everything is impermanent, and that much in life is not personal to us.

- Much of our suffering comes from taking things personally, when events may truly be more about something other than us.

- We build resilience by improving the flexibility of our mind, enabling us to shift perspective and change our vantage point.

- Though it can often appear that other people don't have the problems we have, each of us experiences difficulty and challenge.

CHAPTER 4

Perseverance

Sometimes the challenges we face in life are more like marathons than sprints. If we're resilient, we're able to keep working away at a difficult problem instead of trying to power through it all at once. Resilience gives us the patience to keep going, to persevere through all kinds of obstacles, which then builds even greater resilience. Connecting with our sense of purpose, having realistic plans, and taking small steps are all important strategies that make perseverance possible. Having compassion for ourselves is also key.

Cultivate Perseverance

Perseverance can be thought of as faith in action. In other words, we persevere when we have enough conviction in ourselves and our resourcefulness to know that we can get through the difficulty we're facing. In some ways, perseverance is a basic skill with which we're all born. But it's also an ability we can grow, adding to our well of resilience.

Though we often marvel at natural talent and intelligence and point to them as the cause of a person's success, Stanford University researcher Angela Duckworth, PhD, has championed the concept of *grit*, which she defines as having the passion and perseverance to achieve long-term and meaningful goals and having the direction and commitment to persist in something you feel passionate about. Talent is important, but it's effort that counts for much more.

Whatever our talents, if we don't consciously apply ourselves, that talent goes wasted. It's actually perseverance, in combination with passion, courage, and stamina, that allow us to reach our long-term goals. In a variety of studies, Duckworth and others have demonstrated that sustained application of effort toward a long-term goal is a bigger predictor of success than raw talent. Thus her take-home message: "Talent counts once, effort counts twice."

Grit and perseverance, close cousins if not identical twins, are both related to *agency*. By agency I mean our sense that we *can* do something to impact the outcome of the situation, rather than that we can't. Agency is what drives us to move forward with whatever challenges we face. After all, it's only if we believe we can accomplish something that we will try to take it on. Grit is also related to mindfulness and having a growth mind-set, two concepts mentioned in chapter 3. We can push past setbacks if we have a mind-set that we are capable, and if we use mindfulness to remind ourselves that everything changes and obstacles need not be permanent. In other words, some of the work you're doing to foster flexibility will also strengthen your ability to persevere.

Almost every successful, famous individual had to resist the temptation to quit. Theodor Seuss Geisel's first book had 27 rejections before it was published (you probably know the author better by his pen name, Dr. Seuss). Thomas Edison failed 2,000 times before he created the light bulb. From Oprah to Jerry Seinfeld to J. K. Rowling, stories abound of famous people who got where they are after suffering major setbacks. Where does that kind of perseverance come from? And how can we develop the motivation to keep going, no matter how difficult things get?

Some important theories provide guidance. First, let's consider what psychology researchers call *self-determination theory*. This theory holds that motivation occurs when we act from our own free will, when we are connected to and feel supported by others, and when we have a sense of competency. With those factors in place, we're most motivated when we find value in the activity itself and when it aligns with our sense of purpose. When all that is true, we do things because we want to, as opposed being forced to, a state that's called *intrinsic motivation*. Through several studies, researchers Edward Deci, PhD, and Richard Ryan, PhD, present compelling evidence demonstrating that intrinsically motivated individuals not only have more confidence and persistence, but also perform better and with more creativity. Conversely, when the reward is something extrinsic, for example money, prizes, or acclaim, our motivation tends to be less.

When you consider your own efforts to achieve a goal, perhaps the importance of intrinsic motivation resonates. Let's say you're trying to lose that extra 20 pounds you gained last year. Your doctor wants you to come back and weigh in monthly and tells you about all the bad things that will happen if you don't lose the weight. You feel ashamed and go home and eat a quart of ice cream. That's the impact of extrinsic motivation. Alternatively, you might focus on how good you'll feel about yourself if you lose the weight, how much more energy you'll have, and how much more comfortable you'll be in your clothes. These are things that you value, and they make you want to lose weight. You feel a sense of hope and possibility, and you start going to the gym.

Intentional change theory (ICT), developed by Richard Boyatzis, PhD, is a second way of understanding motivation. It shows that if we want to effect sustainable change and get to our goals, having a vision for where we want to go will powerfully motivate us to create a path forward. Like self-determination theory, ICT emphasizes the importance of having trusting relationships that foster our connectedness. To persevere, we need to lean into others. And we need to lean into our own strengths, tapping into our resourcefulness and inner wisdom.

Though external validation can be helpful, many times we don't get it. But we can always connect with a vision of our ideal self to find the affirmation and nurturing that will motivate us to be at our best. Here's an exercise that will help you access the person you hope to become as a way of tapping into the inner guidance that will help you get where you want to go.

RESILIENCE PRACTICE: Meet Your Future Self

We all have wisdom that resides deep within us, but we don't always learn how to access it. Our inner wisdom can become obscured by the busyness of life, by societal expectations, and by self-criticism. One way to connect with that wisdom is to access a vision of yourself in the future—the best, ideal self that you hope to be one day. Try this exercise when you feel your motivation flagging and you need to strengthen your perseverance so you can reach your goals.

1. Sit in a quiet, comfortable place. Have your journal nearby for the end of the exercise. Close your eyes and imagine that you're walking outside on a beautiful sunny day. You're on a path, walking comfortably.

2. Imagine that the path you're on is taking you to meet your future self, the person that you're becoming. See yourself up ahead, warm and welcoming and very happy to see you.

3. Notice your future self's facial expressions and body language. How do they stand? What are they wearing? Look deeply into their eyes and take in what you see.

4. Move off the path, to a comfortable spot where you can sit as you pose these questions to your future self:

   > What's most important to you in life?

   > What do I need to understand to live a full and meaningful life?

   > What guidance can you provide me regarding the challenge I'm currently facing?

5. Now imagine that your future self has a gift, a special gift that you can take back with you to remind you of this visit and to remind you of who you're becoming. As you accept the gift, ask about its special meaning.

6. Thank your future self for sharing their wisdom and say goodbye in whatever manner feels appropriate. Return to the path that brought you to the meeting, following it in your mind's eye. Walk back in time to the present. When you're ready, gently open your eyes.

7. While it's fresh in your mind, write down as much as you can about who you just met.

   > What were their answers to the questions?

   > What was the gift they gave you? What was its meaning?

CONTINUED

You likely found a deep source of nourishing and reassuring knowledge. Connecting to this resource can be very helpful as you navigate whatever challenges you face.

To continue to tap into this source of inner wisdom, meet with your future self on a regular basis. You can change the setting, inviting them along on your morning commute or meeting over coffee. Discuss whatever is on your mind. See if you can spend time with your future self on a regular basis, building your relationship with this powerful inner ally. Take in the wisdom and experience they share, and let it guide you as you move through your days and weeks.

Goals with a Purpose

We're more likely to persevere in achieving our goals if we're clear about what those goals are and have a plan for achieving them. Knowing what our goals are helps us persevere in the face of adversity (as intentional change theory, mentioned earlier, asserts). Though this sounds straightforward, sometimes we don't approach our challenges in this way. To make consistent progress, it pays to take the time to clarify our objective.

To start, it's critically important to make sure that your goals are aligned with your larger purpose. In other words, what's important to you about achieving this goal? What's your heartfelt reason for doing this? Stepping back and considering what's most important to you in this period of your life can help you see how the task at hand fits in. The more you align your goals with your deep purpose, the easier it will be to stay focused on your path through difficulties and obstacles. That even applies to tasks you'd rather not have to do, or ones that you find yourself avoiding. Staying connected to your sense of purpose is the best motivator for success.

For five years Deidre thought about a novel she wanted to write. Raised Catholic but disheartened by Catholicism's abuse scandals and lack of empowerment for women, she envisioned a story about a woman transcending barriers to establish her voice in the Catholic Church. The subject was close to her heart and she was confident in her ability, yet Deidre had trouble staying on track with the project. As passionate as she was about this topic, she often found it difficult to make time to write. She also found herself lapsing into writer's block. Then she decided to share her goal with her family. With their encouragement, she began writing in earnest, and when she got distracted or struggled with writer's block, her family reminded her of her goal and how important it was to her. Deidre completed her novel and began looking for a publisher.

In Deidre's case, her purpose was clear to herself. She had a message she wanted to impart, a story she wanted to tell. Her persistence over the long term depended on staying connected to that purpose, and she found the help she needed to do just that. But not all of us are as certain of our deep purpose.

As a coach for physicians, I often find myself helping clients reconnect with their deepest purpose so they can move toward their goals. As my clients are all doctors, one might assume that their purpose involves caring for patients. Unfortunately, given the burdens of our complex healthcare system, even physicians can lose their way. One tool I recommend to help people tap into their deepest values is to develop a life purpose statement. These are statements of intent, almost like the mission statement of a company or organization, that help us stay focused and make the decisions that most align with what's of importance to us.

For example, a family physician whom I coached developed this statement:

"I am the passion-driven imaginative healer who listens non-judgmentally, meets people where they are, and connects deeply so that no one has to suffer unnecessarily or alone."

An emergency room physician came up with this:

"I am the wise and fair leader who finds solutions to the puzzle so that all members of the team work together cooperatively to alleviate suffering and create smiles."

And for myself, after reflecting on a long journey to uncover and believe the truth of what occurred in my childhood, I concluded that my purpose has always been to help others find and believe theirs:

"I am the solid-oak healer who helps people find and believe their truth."

These statements help us focus so that we can make decisions that align with our values. You can create a statement of your own. Think about what's most important to you (we'll be doing more of that later in this chapter), and draft a statement using this template:

I am the [describe yourself] *who* [describe what you do] *so that* [describe the "why" of why you do it.]

Here's how it works:

"I am the…" Put a name to the role that you play when engaged in your deepest purpose, along with a descriptor for how you play that role.

Examples: Wise leader, creative problem solver, dependable and loyal protector, patient and encouraging teacher.

"…who…" Define what it is you do in this role. What's most crucial and rewarding for you? What's the task that's at the root of everything important that you do?

Examples: Finds solutions, considers a problem from every angle, works hard to keep people safe, guides students toward confident understanding.

". . .so that. . ." Close the statement by asserting why you do what you do. What's the end goal of what you do in work or life?

Examples:

. . . so that all members of the team work together cooperatively to alleviate suffering and create smiles.

. . . to ease the burden of whoever comes to me for help.

. . . so everyone can live their lives without fear or distress.

. . . to prepare them for the challenges and opportunities ahead of them.

Try it! There are no wrong answers. You'll find that this statement can act as a powerful guide when you're facing challenges or difficult crossroads.

Schedules and Steps

In addition to connecting with your purpose, perseverance depends on setting realistic and specific short-term milestones of progress as you move toward long-term goals. Before we try an exercise that connects your goals to an action plan, here are some important elements of planning to keep in mind whenever you're trying to reach an important objective.

A timeline. Imagine deciding to run a marathon or compete in a triathlon. To have any hope of being physically and mentally prepared for the event, you'd need to map out how many miles of running you have to do every week and follow that schedule closely. Develop a timeline for any project to make sure that you always know what you need to do next. It will also help you pace yourself.

Schedules and checklists. Have you ever noticed that when you check something off your to-do list, you feel a sense of contentment and satisfaction? It's not your imagination—neuroscience studies show us that completing a task and checking it off a list actually triggers a surge of *dopamine*, one of the brain's chemical messengers that give us a feeling of well-being. Create milestones for your project, and each time you check one off, you'll give yourself a dose of feeling good.

Small steps. It's always helpful to approach an ambitious goal in a series of small, doable steps. Try to do something regularly that moves you toward your goals, even if it only seems like a tiny accomplishment. Instead of focusing on how unachievable a far-off goal seems, ask yourself, "What's one thing I know I can accomplish today that helps me move in the direction I want to go?" In Deidre's example, she might decide to write 500 words each day, or spend an hour every morning writing.

A small start. If your goal was to run a marathon, but you hadn't been exercising much, you wouldn't practice by running the whole distance the first time out. You'd find a training program that began with running a short distance first, or even walking, so you wouldn't overextend, get injured, and give up early on. Starting small makes a large task feel more manageable, and it gives you a small victory right from the beginning.

A realistic assessment. Perseverance works best when your goal is a realistic one for your unique life circumstance. That's not to say you can't aim for something challenging and outside your comfort zone, like writing a novel or reaching a savings goal. But if you have three kids under the age of 10 and a busy full-time job, this might not be the time to build that log cabin with your own hands like you've always wanted. Instead, why not schedule a fun fall foliage weekend at a cabin, where you can get ideas to use when the time does come? Our goals vary at different points in our life, and that's perfectly fine.

RESILIENCE PRACTICE: What's Important to You?

Staying motivated to achieve our goals requires understanding why those goals are important to us. Reaching a goal inevitably requires making trade-offs—giving up some things so we can focus on what matters most. Knowing what's important makes that balancing act easier, enabling us to say no to distractions. This exercise will help you use the values that matter most to you as a starting point in achieving your goals. Use your journal to record your answers to the questions.

1. Let's start by considering your values. Think about the qualities you demonstrate when you're at your best (for example honesty, integrity, growth) and identify a moment in the past when, looking back, you are particularly proud of how you acted. This moment could be from an event at work or with family—any time where you really shone. Take a moment to list the values that emerged during this event.

    My top values are:

2. Identify a goal you'd like to achieve, one that you feel is practical, is attainable, and leads you in the direction of the values you listed. Write this goal down.

3. Now ask yourself these questions:

    What's important to me about this goal?

    What's my heartfelt reason for pursuing it?

    How does this goal align with my values?

    What will I need to do less of to reach this goal? What will I need to say no to?

CONTINUED

Example: Beth values her career; one of her proudest moments is planning an ad campaign that came in under budget and performed beyond expectations. She writes "creative thinking," "teamwork," and "being challenged" as her top values. The goal she wants to achieve is to leave her job and start a business of her own. This is important to her because she'll have more freedom to do the creative and challenging work that she likes.

4. Now let's create an action plan.

> What small steps will you need to take to improve your chances of reaching your goal? List these.
>
> When will you take these steps? Set a timeline.
>
> Which step will you take today? Tomorrow?

Example: To achieve her goal, Beth will need to find mentors to guide her. The steps she lists are to identify knowledgeable people in her industry, make contact with them, and build a support network to help her start her new venture.

5. List any current habits or practices to which you can connect those new steps.

Example: Beth decides that for the next month she'll spend part of her lunch hour each day doing research and send one email every morning to someone she wants to meet.

Remember, even for the biggest of goals, every small decision and action you take will help you get closer to success.

Accepting Life's Obstacles

Life throws us lots of curveballs from all directions. We may be moving forward on a big life project only to have an unexpected turn of events take front stage: an aging parent needing care, a child struggling at school, understaffing at work, a public health emergency. How can we possibly stay on course and persevere?

Perseverance doesn't mean ignoring reality. If anything, it's the opposite: In order to overcome any setback, we first have to accept that it exists. It's always helpful to remind ourselves that we all veer off our path—it's just the nature of life. Recall the first mark of existence, which basically boils down to the fact that stuff happens. Though we may have decided it's the right time to work on a big project, life may have different plans for us. If you think back on your life, you can probably see that your own journey has not been a linear one. In fact, on our way to visit a beautiful mountain, it's not unusual to come across difficult terrain that lies between us and the peak. Maybe we didn't plan for the difficult terrain and no one told us it would be there, yet we have to traverse it to get where we're going regardless.

Simply accepting the reality of our circumstances can be an incredibly productive step. We can spend a lot of energy resisting or railing against something—whether it's something internal, like a personality trait, challenging emotion, or physical pain, or an external factor, like bad timing or difficult circumstances. This reaction can leave us worrying, replaying events and conversations over and over in our mind, stuck and upset because of what's occurring. We can't move forward with perseverance because until we accept the situation, we're just going around in circles.

That principle is underscored in a form of therapy called *acceptance and commitment therapy* (ACT), which affirms that living our most vital life involves accepting reality as it is and working with whatever that brings us. With that acceptance comes the understanding that life is full of choice points.

Perseverance involves facing problems head-on so you can commit to choices that align with your values and decrease your struggle and distress. Here's an example.

> A successful fashion designer, Jacinta put her career on hold after a car accident left her with chronic leg pain. She'd been to doctor after doctor, tried medication after medication, yet the pain remained. On some days, she felt fine. On others, she felt like her leg was in a vise. She lived in constant fear that the pain would return, worrying what each day would bring. She frequently told herself that if only the pain would go away, she could continue to pursue her career, but that otherwise "I can't do anything useful or enjoyable because of my pain."
>
> After working with an ACT therapist, Jacinta realized that many of her thoughts were amplifying her suffering and that she'd been caught in a life that was overly focused on the pain. She realized that though her pain was a difficult burden, when she accepted the uncertainty it brought, she was freer to commit to the importance of her career. This wasn't easy, but acceptance helped her make the daily choices necessary to pursue what was deeply important to her. She began to understand that the pain was like the difficult terrain that lay between her and the beautiful mountain of her goals.

Jacinta was doing more than learning to work with her physical pain. She was also giving up a belief that her life should be a certain way. In a sense, she was stepping away from denying the reality of her situation and stepping into the truth of her life circumstances. Doing so did not mean giving up on hope for less pain. Instead, it allowed her to persevere, managing the pain *and* pursuing her life goals, instead of expending energy railing against her misfortune. Her hope became aligned with what was possible, which helped her persevere in the face of difficulty.

Consider for a moment ways you've fought with a reality that kept you from your goals. We all do this. In my case, I spent years fighting my own history, telling myself how unfair life had been, thinking about how much better my life would have been if only the events of my childhood hadn't happened. It wasn't until I faced the fact that my past was unchangeably what it was that I could truly embrace and be fully open to the many good things my life has included.

To close this chapter, I'd like to coach you to stay on course and persevere as you pursue what's most deeply important to you. In that spirit, I hope you'll try this next resilience practice.

RESILIENCE PRACTICE: Setting Intentions

You're likely familiar with New Year's resolutions. These goals are often black and white: Either you achieve them or you don't. And if you don't, well, that never feels very good, does it? An approach that promotes perseverance involves setting intentions instead of making resolutions. Intentions help us see our path forward, whether it's toward a specific goal, like losing weight, or a broader change, like being kinder to ourselves and others.

Intentions work because they help us direct our attention. Without intention, it's easy for our focus to wander away from our goals, leaving us prone to all sorts of distractions, from surfing the Internet to binge-watching a show to chatting with co-workers instead of finishing aproject. Intentions keep us on course, providing direction for our efforts, helping us focus on what's most

CONTINUED

important to us that day, week, month, or year. They help us persevere toward our aspirations and overcome hurdles that arise.

This practice will help you set an intention for your day. You can do this first thing in the morning if that's convenient, or on the bus, subway, or car ride to work. You only need two to five uninterrupted minutes. (You can use your journal for this exercise if you like, or just do it in your head.) As you set your intention, trust in your inner knowledge of what's most important to you and what goals align with who you are at your best.

1. First, consider these questions:

   What is it that matters most to you at this point in your life?

   What is it that truly makes you happy?

   What nourishes you and gives you a sense of meaning?

2. Second, with these answers in mind, think about what you can do today that aligns you with these important factors.

   To start, you might choose an intention related to an attitude you aspire to, such as:

   Be more kind

   Be less reactive with your kids or partner

   Experience more gratitude

   Be a positive role model for others

   Have more compassion toward yourself

Alternatively, your intention could be a very specific and practical one, such as:

Keep your house tidier

Incorporate more exercise in your life

Eat fewer sweets

Perform random acts of kindness

Meditate regularly

3. At the end of the day, review the intention you set and consider if your actions served those intentions. Don't judge yourself for missed opportunities—simply decide to keep doing your best. Make notes about this in your journal if you like.

The wonderful thing about intentions is that whereas goals are future oriented, intentions can be achieved moment to moment. We can satisfy an intention right now, giving us an instant of success toward our goal. Intentions can provide a positive motivation for change. Instead of being something to beat yourself up about, an intention can serve as your guiding light.

KEY TAKEAWAYS

- To persevere, it's critical that we build and maintain our motivation.

- Though society would have us believe that it's talent and intelligence that are most important for success, in truth "talent counts once and effort counts twice."

- We are most motivated when we find value in an activity itself, it aligns with our sense of purpose, and we do it because we want to as opposed to being forced to.

- Breaking tasks into tiny steps is key. Ask yourself, "What's one thing I can accomplish today that will move me forward?"

- Accepting the reality of our circumstances frees up the energy lost on resisting or railing against our circumstances.

- Setting a daily intention helps us align with our purpose.

CHAPTER 5

Self-Regulation

Not only is life a balancing act, it's one we have to manage while events rush at us like waves in the ocean, and our own thoughts and emotions sometimes race out of control. With so many demands competing for our attention, to be resilient we need to pace ourselves and learn to regulate how we react to the challenges life sends our way. In this chapter we'll explore ways to self-regulate, so you can keep calm, handle difficult emotions, and channel your energy in positive directions.

Cultivate Self-Regulation

In the previous chapter, we learned that our motivation is strongest when we're acting by our own choice. Whereas we have no control over the unexpected obstacles that arise in our life, we *do* have a choice in how we react to them. So many times we forget this simple truth: No matter what we face, there is always a moment of choice. There's an oft-cited quote that brings this point home: "Between stimulus and response there is a space. In that space lies our freedom and our power to choose our response. In our response lies our growth and our happiness."

Often, however, we're so busy that we're blind to these choice points. We rush around putting out fires, managing all sorts of difficulties, experiencing so many emotions that we're caught up in a tailspin. It can all feel out of control, almost as if we're being run by our lives instead of the other way around. With resilience, we can self-regulate more effectively. We can take a pause, remove our blinders, and see that moment of choice. And we can exert our agency in choosing our next step. Here's one example.

> Jake, a 47-year-old surgeon, came to see me for coaching after having angry outbursts in the operating room (OR). He was a highly respected surgeon but had received multiple complaints from nurses about his condescending and belittling approach. One incident involved a nurse just out of training who had always wanted to work in the OR. After she struggled to locate an instrument Jake needed, Jake lashed out at her, shouting "How dare you think you're good enough to be in my OR?" The nurse began crying and ran out of the room, deeply distraught.
>
> Luckily, Jake was eager to do better. I had him tune in to his emotional temperature, getting to know the physical warning signs of rising anger and frustration. It took some practice, but Jake began to notice that when his anger was taking over, his breathing became shallower and his

face became warm. Furthermore, his whole body tightened, almost as though he was bracing for a fight. Once he learned to recognize these signs, he was able to see how much agency he truly had to manage his anger. He was then able to bring his emotions under greater control, developing the same mastery over them that he displayed with difficult surgical cases.

You might think that Jake was a stereotypical brusque and uncaring surgeon, but in fact he was a compassionate individual who valued kindness and respect. He simply didn't know how to regulate himself. And under stress, Jake's raw emotions sometimes emerged. Though his medical training had involved 11 years of study beyond college, it had included next to nothing about self-regulation. Further, he hadn't learned to take into account the impact his lack of emotional management had on those around him. As he aligned his actions with his values, however, the eruptions of anger became much less frequent.

The heightened awareness that Jake developed was, in fact, the first stage of what's known as *emotional intelligence*, that is, the ability to understand and regulate one's emotions. In his bestselling book of that title, psychologist and science journalist Dan Goleman, PhD, unpacks the topic, discussing why it matters. He explains that the goal of cultivating emotional intelligence is not to free us of emotions, but to grant us the full range of emotions and experiences, including the more difficult ones. Along with that comes the choice to act in ways that are concordant with our values and our goals. In other words, when we develop our emotional intelligence, we're not trying to stop the flow of our emotions. Instead we're trying to respond to them with greater agility. Emotional intelligence allows us to self-regulate even when we feel overwhelmed by our emotions.

Many of us haven't developed our emotional intelligence because we've been taught that emotions are to be avoided, or that some emotions are acceptable and others are not. Even the commonplace "How are you? I'm fine" discourse in which we all engage can lead us to believe that emotions have no place in our day-to-day interactions. Societal messaging about emotions runs strong, and it's often negative. We're all familiar with phrases such as "Big boys don't cry," or "We don't do anger in this family. Go to your room and come out when you've got a smile on your face," or "Just get over it!" So we learn to put our emotions away. Yet whether at work or at home, in close relationships or with strangers, if we can develop more ease with our emotions, then we will likely find that they exert less control over us.

How do we do so? Here are three important principles that can help.

1. **Learn your triggers.** Emotional intelligence begins with under-standing what triggers strong emotional reactions in us. Our emotions can be triggered by many things, but especially common triggers include:

   - Feeling that someone is not respecting us
   - Sensing that we're not being listened to
   - Not having our needs appreciated
   - Being treated unfairly or witnessing unfairness toward others

   Even in the best of families, many of us experienced these triggers in our childhood. Back then, we were innocent and vulnerable; we depended on our parents to meet our needs, but they didn't always get it quite right. As adults, circumstances can take us back to those vulnerable moments, and we can be hit with a rush of emotions like those from the past.

2. **Be kind.** Self-compassion is an ongoing theme when it comes to building resilience, so this bears mentioning again: Be kind to yourself. It can be painful when strong emotions are triggered, but there's nothing wrong with us for experiencing them. Our emotions are simply part of being human. Remember, it's our response that we control, not the emotions themselves.

3. **Know they will pass.** Remember the second mark of existence from chapter 3? Everything is impermanent, and that's especially true for emotions, which typically pass in one to two minutes. When you recall this, it will increase your sense of safety as you let your emotions be present. Though they can feel so powerful that we wonder if we can survive, if we stay grounded we can watch our emotions arise, pass through us, and fade away.

When strong emotions take hold, we need tools to remain in the here and now. Here's an exercise that will teach you to use your breathing to stay anchored in the present, so your emotions won't carry you away.

RESILIENCE PRACTICE:
STOP and Gain Perspective

Our emotions can feel so powerful that they overwhelm us, clouding our judgment and making it hard for us to accurately appraise what's going on. We lose the clarity to see what we need in that moment and choose what's best to do next. By calming the emotional storm and seeing how the situation looks from the stance of an observer, we can become clear-sighted again, gaining the perspective and freedom to consider our options. Practice this STOP technique and use it any time you feel your emotions running away with you.

To practice, bring to mind a stressful situation in which you've found yourself. Don't pick one that's 10 out of 10 on your stress meter—instead, go for something that's more in the 3 to 5 range. Imagine that you're in that situation right now. Then follow these steps:

CONTINUED

S: STOP everything you're doing; hit the pause button and still yourself. Freeze the frame.

T: TAKE three slow deep breaths. Focus on the sensations of breathing and feel your body slowing down.

O: OBSERVE yourself and your circumstances. Imagine that you've stepped out of yourself and are observing the situation from the stance of a neutral third party. Be an observer who has a great deal of compassion for you and what you're going through. From this vantage point, what does the observer see?

P: PRAISE yourself in any way you can, small or large. Remind yourself of your strengths. Congratulate yourself for choosing to de-escalate this situation. Then think about what your next step should be, now that your mind is clearer.

When you're ready, reflect on this practice. Did you see your situation in a different light? If so, what shifted? Did you discover any new options for how to handle it?

Taking the stance of an observer is a vital tool for self-regulation, generating the calm we need to take effective action. Like everything, it takes practice. Try this exercise out a few times this week, and soon you'll be able to call on it whenever you need to.

Deal with Your Feelings

Emotions are at the heart of being human. Love, sadness, joy, grief, fear, surprise, hope—they're all the stuff of Shakespearean plays and more, yet we learn little about how to manage them. We're uncomfortable with sadness, grief, anger, and fear. We brace ourselves, hoping these "negative" emotions will rapidly depart. At other times, we embrace joy, love, and elation, hanging on tightly and hoping they will never end.

We typically don't learn moderation in dealing with our emotions; either we try to push them completely away, afraid of their intensity, or we let them overtake us and regret our actions afterward. But as you've seen with the STOP technique, it is possible to weather the storms of intense emotion. When we pause and observe our emotions, we begin to see that they're simply a part of our human landscape. Like clouds in the sky, they form and pass by. The self-regulation that comes with resilience enables us to suspend judgment about the emotions we experience, and simply let them be present. Let's consider three common emotions that can be hard to handle and discuss how to work with them.

Anger

Of all our emotions, anger probably has the worst reputation. Many of us saw poor role modeling of anger in our families. Perhaps we witnessed anger that was kept bottled up, then exploded in a parental argument over the dinner table, or at night when we were supposed to be sleeping. Those kind of scenarios don't teach us much about how best to manage our own anger. We end up trying to repress our anger, and it inevitably sneaks up on us and bursts out when we least expect it. Here are some strategies to help you self-regulate your anger.

Look for the influences. It can be liberating to understand what drives our anger; often there are specific factors that leave us prone to an angry reaction. For some, overdoses of violence in the form of movies, news media, and other graphic content primes us to respond angrily. Lack of sleep and lack of attention to our own needs can also play a part. If you're struggling with anger issues, think of your mind as a garden planted with the seeds of various emotions. Are you watering the seeds of anger and fear by overdosing on upsetting news reports and violent images? Is lack of self-care making it difficult to water seeds of patience and understanding? How can you water the seeds of kindness and calm instead?

Cool down before you act. Sometimes anger comes with a strong sense of being hurt, and we quickly move to a feeling of spite: If you've made me suffer, I'm going to get you back and make you suffer even more. Sadly, this cycle of reactivity simply causes more damage. The Zen master and peace activist Thich Nhat Hanh likens anger within us to our house being on fire. "If your house is on fire," he says, "the most urgent thing to do is to go back and try to put out the fire, not to run after the person you believe to be the arsonist." In other words, the wisest response to anger is cooling one's own flames. Taking a pause and focusing on our breathing is a powerful tool for doing this. Rely on the STOP technique, or simply take slow deep breaths and acknowledge what you're feeling: *Breathing in, I'm experiencing anger. Breathing out, I'm experiencing anger.* Continue until you feel the emotion passing.

Avoid one-sided conversations. When someone harms us, it's easy to slip into a loud imagined tête-à-tête in which we tell that person off, usually in frank and heated language. But this doesn't impact the person we're upset with, and just leaves us suffering from unprocessed anger. A better idea, once you've cooled the flames, is to have a calm conversation in real life, explaining why you were upset.

Fear

Fear can be a bigger driver of our behavior than we realize. When we pay attention, we can see how often we're motivated by fear of messing up, fear of being blamed, and fear of being shamed because of our actions or inaction. Keep these points in mind to manage your fears effectively.

Accept it. As with anger, the unpleasantness of fear leads us to resist it, bracing against it and trying to push it away. But doing this only prolongs and feeds our fear. The better path is to stay present with our fear, allowing the emotion to exist and reminding ourselves that it will pass. This helps the emotion move through us more rapidly and with less duress.

Reach out. One reason that we adults avoid facing our fear is that fear can make us feel like a child again, crouching in a corner, afraid of the bogeyman in the closet. Fear makes us vulnerable and causes us to feel at risk and destabilized. But a frightened child needs attention and comfort, and that's also what's called for when we're gripped by fear in adulthood. The surest antidote for fear is connection and compassion. Reach out to someone when you feel fear overwhelming you, and be sure to attend to the social connection practices in chapter 2.

For years after my childhood trauma was past, my nights were interrupted by fear and often outright terror. I'd lay in bed curled up in a ball, feeling small and bracing for what my mind feared was to come. It took many years to understand that all my bracing and resisting actually fed my fear demons. As counterintuitive as it seems, I eventually learned that staying present with fear was the way to lessen its hold on my psyche. As with anger, simply letting the emotion be present, and reminding ourselves that it will pass, helps it move through us more rapidly and with less duress. Though greeting fear with something like "hello, fear" may sound juvenile, it beats quivering in a corner with our amygdala activated and the stress response eroding our mental and physical health. Instead of pushing the fear away, we remind ourselves that we can manage it. Just as we do with a small child experiencing fear, we acknowledge the suffering in ourselves and attend to it.

Sadness

Sadness is almost the inverse of anger and fear; it seems to pull us inward rather than carry us away. Most of us learned to stay away from sadness, taught that if we give in to it we'll be dragged down, down, down, ending up like Eeyore, the downtrodden donkey from *Winnie-the-Pooh*. Yet sadness is simply another emotion, one of the many that we can experience as a normal part of our lives. Consider these simple but more effective responses to sadness.

Feel it. If we try to steer clear of sadness, what happens? Whether it's someone struggling with the impact of a difficult diagnosis or grief and sadness following the loss of an important relationship or death of a loved one, I've seen over and over that when sadness is pushed away, it limits our ability to experience joy. And far from vanishing from our consciousness, sadness sometimes emerges as anger or even rage.

Express it. Remember the second mark of human existence: Everything shifts and changes. In other words, we can remind ourselves that sadness will pass. I've found that when I let my own sadness be present and even have a good cry, it almost always passes with greater calm and ease than if I'd tried to remain stoic.

Our emotions can catch us off guard. We've all had the experience of going from completely calm to lashing out in a matter of seconds. It can feel almost like a switch has been flipped. Your boss hands you an extra assignment the day before you're off to a much-needed vacation; your spouse forgets your anniversary; your child refuses to eat the dinner you labored over. And you go from zero to ninety in what feels like a heartbeat. It can be helpful to realize that there's a name for this: *limbic hijack*. It happens when our brain senses a threat and kicks our fight/ flight/freeze instinct into high gear. Within moments, we find ourselves reacting with spite and anger, usually inflaming the situation.

In her book *Radical Compassion*, mindfulness educator Tara Brach, PhD, describes a practice called RAIN, which can help you manage difficult emotions and avoid being hijacked by them.

RESILIENCE PRACTICE: RAIN Technique

We learn little about how to sit with our emotions; we're more likely to try to push them away. But the more we do so, the more they persist. In the RAIN exercise, we become more comfortable with our emotions by allowing them to be present. When a difficult or unpleasant emotion arises, if you have the capacity, try following these steps; if possible, conduct the exercise in a quiet place where you can sit comfortably.

R: Recognize what is happening. Bring to mind a difficulty you're experiencing. Looking inward, ask yourself: *What's my inner experience? What's here right now? What's calling for my attention?* Let yourself recognize whatever is present, whether it's fear, anger, sadness, or any other feeling.

A: Allow the experience. Next, see if you can allow the feelings to be present just as they are. This can feel difficult, and you may worry that you'll be overwhelmed by the feelings. Your mind may begin judging, fixing, problem-solving. Your task, though, is to simply let what's here be here. Remind yourself that you are safe, and that you can handle whatever arises. Remind yourself that all feelings pass.

I: Investigate with interest and care. Now explore what's going on in your body as you consider this difficulty. With a sense of curiosity, check in with yourself, as kindly and gently as you can. Scan yourself slowly from head to toe, and note if there are areas of tightness or tension, warmth or ease. See if you can greet whatever you find with compassion.

N: Nurture with self-compassion. Finally, bring nurturance to your entire experience. Imagine a loving presence who's telling you, "It's okay. You'll be all right. I'm here for you." This may be yourself, a beloved person, or a spiritual entity. It could be a scene from nature or simply a sense of light and ease. Take a few slow deep breaths, taking in this sense of comfort and care.

CONTINUED

Having done this exercise, notice any shifts in your physical state. Notice whether you feel calmer. Let yourself sit still for another minute or two and rest, taking in this state rather than quickly jumping back into your day. You may feel like you've had a very gentle rain wash over you.

The Power of Pausing

Do you ever feel like your life is passing you by? That you're running, running, running to keep up, and there's barely a moment to stop? Modern life can be incredibly busy, with demands, tasks, texts, and responsibilities galore. Sometimes there's a seemingly endless to-do list. And often we're expected to be available 24/7, without time to reflect, calm, or even pause. This comes at quite a cost to us and affects our ability to manage our emotions, which sometimes come in rapid fire when we're too busy to pay attention to them. We push them away, then they spring out and derail us when we don't expect them.

Stopping and pausing can powerfully shift this imbalance, enabling us to self-regulate effectively. A simple pause, even for the time it takes to have three deep breaths, helps us reset. We create a space where we can remind ourselves: "Even if my to-do list is long, and I have much on my plate, I'm okay right now and I will be okay going forward. I *can* manage what I have to get done." It may not seem like much, but like micro-moments of connection (chapter 2), brief breaks in our activity can have a big impact on our well-being.

In fact, scheduled breaks are now considered so important to successful leadership that something called the *purposeful pause* is commonly taught in business school courses. Janice Marturano, founder of the Institute for Mindful Leadership, has noted that when business leaders incorporate purposeful pauses into their days, they experience greater innovation, clarity, and productivity.

A purposeful pause can help us in many ways. It involves intentionally stopping whatever we're doing, mentally and physically, interrupting our current pattern of thinking and behavior, and checking in with ourselves to see what's truly there. So often we operate on a kind of autopilot, not fully aware of what we're doing. A purposeful pause takes us out of autopilot and into full waking consciousness. From there, the view is often refreshingly clear.

> Avani, the CEO of a midsized manufacturing company, found that her workdays were spent running from one high-stakes meeting to another, with no time to process each meeting or to develop a strategy for coping with her load. She'd been working this way since taking the job three years earlier, and the stress was taking its toll. She was exhausted and experienced increasingly frequent stomach pain that made her wonder if she was getting an ulcer.
>
> She decided to schedule purposeful pauses in her day, planned breaks when she would stop working, bring her mind to the present moment, and spend several minutes simply noticing her thoughts and feelings, and the environment around her. Soon Avani found that purposeful pauses helped her to reflect, allowing her to gauge the right steps in her busy workdays. Pausing also gave Avani a greater sense of calm, allowing her mind to move out of the weeds of day-to-day pressures and into a much-needed bigger picture perspective. She began taking a purposeful pause between every meeting on her schedule. Soon her feelings of stress lessened and her stomach pain disappeared.

Like Avani, when we pause what we're doing, we can better see what's truly going on around us and determine the most important thing for us to attend to next. Stepping back, we can stop and see: This is what's important to me here. We can also savor the good in what's happening in the present moment. Pausing helps us observe the joy and richness that are often present in the most ordinary moments of our days.

A purposeful pause can be created anytime simply by stopping and taking a few slow deep breaths. It can also take the form of a walk around the block, a brief meditation, getting some exercise, immersion in a hobby, or simply taking a coffee break. The important point is to create time and space to allow your mind to quiet down and then reflect with greater clarity and calm.

In addition, there are specific situations in which a pause can be particularly helpful. If you're anticipating a difficult conversation or situation or you have a difficult decision to make, take a moment to stop and take three slow deep breaths. In moments when you have too much to do, try taking a pause. Pay attention to the calm that enters. I've found that when I'm feeling overwhelmed, pausing almost always helps me regroup and see that things are actually manageable. And manageable always beats overwhelming.

Nowhere is pausing more important than in our personal relationships. It's with the people closest to us that we can find our emotions most easily triggered, and where we tend to be at our most reactive. It's also where the cost of an unchecked reaction to our emotions is highest. Perhaps you can recall moments where your internal temperature rapidly rose, and in the heat of the moment you came out with a spiteful barb that you later regretted. Like many parents, I can recall times when my son was a teenager and I countered his emotional reactivity with reactivity of my own. Learning to take pauses was a critical part of shifting this harmful pattern, and the payoff in building a more respectful and trusting relationship was enormous.

Sometimes it's relatively easy to take a break and pull our attention from whatever we've been engaged with. Many times, however, our patterns of thought, emotion, and behavior are too deeply rooted. When you find it more difficult to do this, or you want a more structured separation from the activities of the day, try this exercise.

RESILIENCE PRACTICE: Mindfulness Meditation

One way to take a purposeful pause during a busy time is with a brief meditation. Whether you can find five minutes or fifteen, this exercise in mindful meditation will help you bring your attention to the present moment, quieting your mind, reducing the pull of emotions, and helping you gain clarity around the choices you have in how you interact with whatever is going on in your life.

1. Begin by sitting comfortably in a relaxed position on a chair, a cushion, or the floor. Allow your hands to rest comfortably in your lap. Let your shoulders drop and your forehead unfurrow. Try to relax the area around your eyes.

2. Bring your attention to your breathing, not breathing any differently but simply connecting with your breath. Feel the sensations of breathing, one breath at a time. When one breath ends, notice the sensation of the next breath beginning.

3. Keep your attention on your breathing. As your mind wanders, notice that your attention has strayed—you can mentally note "thinking" or "wandering" in a soft internal whisper—then gently redirect your attention right back to your breathing. Don't try to suppress or judge your thoughts, just let them fade. If your mind gets lost in worries about your to-do list, remind yourself that all you have to do is take one small step in meeting the workload you face. That's all. Just one small step.

4. Stay focused on your breathing for at least five minutes, sitting silently, connecting to your breath. When time is up, be sure to give yourself some appreciation for doing this practice today.

KEY TAKEAWAYS

- Though we can't control the situations life throws at us, we always have a choice in how we react to them.

- Anger can be fueled by overdoses of violence in the form of movies, news media, and other imagery, or by lack of sleep and lack of attention to our own needs.

- Fear of messing up, being blamed for something, or being shamed is often what drives the actions and words we later regret.

- When we're afraid, we're like a vulnerable child crouching in a corner, scared of the bogeyman. The antidote to fear is connection, comfort, and compassion.

- The practice of RAIN builds our capacity to sit with discomfort, bringing a nurturing presence to whatever difficulty we face.

- Stopping and pausing can bring calm and clarity to the most stressful day, even if we don't think we have the time to do so.

- A pause can be created by stopping and taking a few slow deep breaths, walking around the block, doing a brief meditation, exercising, diving into a hobby, or simply taking a coffee break.

CHAPTER 6

Positivity

More than just a happy face, positive emotions and optimism contribute to good mental and physical health, and build our resilience to the hardships we encounter. Traditionally, the science of psychology has focused heavily on deficits and pathology in an effort to understand mental illness and find effective treatments. But more recently, research scientists have put long-overdue attention toward exploring and understanding the role strengths and proficiencies play in allowing us to thrive and succeed. As a result, there's more evidence than ever that positivity brings widespread gains to mind and body.

Cultivate Positivity

Over the past few decades, we've seen a sea change in how researchers in the field of psychology approach the study of human nature. A new approach to studying human behavior began in the 1990s when researcher Martin Seligman, PhD, illuminated a major flaw in prior psychological theories: They focused on what humans do poorly but paid little attention to what humans do well. This fostered a belief that focusing on deficits would illuminate a path to wellness, and that dwelling on negative qualities helps people strengthen and improve.

In fact, the opposite is true. Following Seligman's lead, a new field of study called *positive psychology* emerged. And its investigations show us that to understand optimal human functioning, looking at strengths and what we're doing well is vitally important. Yet even in our own lives, many of us focus heavily on our weaknesses and deficits, often with the belief that doing so is what's needed to motivate us to improve. But is this true? Let's try a brief exercise:

Bring to mind anything challenging that's on your to-do list. Then list the ways you might think you're not up for the challenge. For example:

I'm not good at this.

Others are so much better at this than I am.

I'll never get this done.

Now rate your level of motivation to complete the task on a scale from 0 (no motivation) to 10 (highly motivated).

Next imagine the same task, but this time tell yourself affirming messages, describing why you're exactly the right person to get this done. For example:

I'm great at doing this kind of thing.

I may procrastinate but I always get things done.

I have just the right skills and strengths to do this.

Then re-rate your level of motivation and see if your score goes up or down.

Most people find the second approach considerably more inspiring, thus validating the idea that focusing on our strengths and skills is a more effective motivator. Somewhat paradoxically, the more we focus on what we're not doing well or what still needs to get done, the more draining and daunting our tasks can seem. The more we focus on our successes and what we're doing right, the more confidence and energy we have to accomplish our tasks.

More than 500 published studies have documented the connection between positive emotions and success across multiple life domains. But positivity's effect goes beyond motivating us to succeed. In the physical realm, positive emotions have been shown to increase immune function, lower cortisol and other stress hormones, reduce inflammatory response to stress, and increase resistance to cold viruses. In terms of mental health, our ability to generate positive emotions increases confidence and enhances effective coping, sociability, and self-efficacy, all of which actively help move us toward our goals.

Positivity makes us resilient, but not because we put on a happy face and push anything difficult under the carpet. To the contrary, true positivity works when we allow ourselves to have a balance between up and down emotional states.

By "down," we're talking about what most consider to be negative emotions—fear, anxiety, anger, grief, sadness, and the like. These have their place. Anxiety can improve our ability to solve problems. Fear points us to danger. Anger alerts us to injustice. Grief points to our connectedness with others. Sadness reminds us of what's important to us. As we discussed in chapter 5, resilience depends on self-regulation, which includes allowing every emotion its place and not pushing any away. The more we push negative emotions away, the more they're likely to return and blindside us.

Positivity is not a practice of suppressing or denying those negative feelings, but rather is one of seeking and supporting positive emotions such as love, joy, hope, and gratitude. These emotions activate the *rest and digest* system, fueling upward spirals of health, well-being, and cognition. These spirals broaden our visual focus, attention, and thoughts, leading to greater creativity, flexibility, inclusivity, and problem-solving. Known as the *broaden-and-build* model, this explains why positive states help us cope with stress.

Just as knowing the importance of diet and exercise helps motivate us to make healthier choices, understanding the role of positivity in our wellness can also bring us to a healthier state. Let's look at this in action.

> Monica had long struggled with anxiety. She grew up in poverty, with her family often scrambling to pay rent, and moving numerous times due to periods of homelessness. This insecurity had driven many of Monica's life decisions, including dropping out of high school because she felt like she didn't fit in. Now struggling to find a stable job, her mind was often consumed with fear, rumination, and worry about what would happen next. Seeing that her anxiety was getting the best of her, Monica's job counselor worked with her to help Monica see how a more positive vantage point could benefit her. She began by making a daily list of things she was grateful for, and she took time to savor at least one experience every day. Over a period of months, Monica found that her mind gravitated more naturally from fear and worry toward the things in her life that were truly going well. She became motivated and better able to present herself as a more desirable candidate for employment, and eventually landed the stable job she hoped for.

Like Monica, you can use the power of gratitude as your entry point to a more positive outlook.

RESILIENCE PRACTICE:
Building Positivity with Gratitude

Building your positivity won't stop the daily obstacles and challenges you face, but it will add to your resilience, helping you cope with challenges small and large. Positive emotions bring many mental and physical benefits, including an improved ability to solve problems and master whatever difficulties appear in your life. Cultivating gratitude is one of the most powerful strategies to connect with positive emotions.

For this exercise, take a few minutes to think of someone who helped you in times of difficulty. This can be a teacher or mentor, a friend, or simply someone who gave you practical assistance with a difficult situation right when you needed it.

Now write a brief letter to this person. Tell them what they did to help you and how their actions affected you. Be as specific as you can. Take a moment to update them about your current challenges and how their actions help you today. Don't worry about finding the perfect words or using correct grammar and spelling, as that's not what's important here.

Read your letter to yourself, paying attention to how you feel when you experience gratitude. Take note of any positive physical sensations: Do you feel your face or body growing warmer? Are you more relaxed?

If it feels comfortable, plan a visit with this individual to express your thanks. Alternatively, you can send them the letter. But you don't have to do either, as simply writing the letter provides you with the positive emotions that replenish your resilience well.

Whenever you're stressed about an issue or challenge, try leaning into gratitude, either with this exercise or by simply taking note of things you're grateful for.

Challenging Negativity

Perhaps you've heard that human beings suffer from something called the *negativity bias*. The idea is that negative thoughts and experiences are like Velcro to our minds—they stick easily—whereas positive ones are more like Teflon and often quickly slip away. In other words, the human mind is biased toward the negative. Neuroscience research confirms that the human brain is more alert to negative events than positive ones. Like our response to stress (chapter 1), it's thought that this is an evolutionary phenomenon: For our ancestors, scanning for danger was a matter of life and death. But how does the negativity bias play out in modern times?

Unfortunately, similarly to the way our stress response can be problematic, our tendency to focus on the negative puts us on high alert when we don't need to be. We dwell on insults, fixate on mistakes, and pay greater attention to what isn't going well than to what is. In our social interactions, this bias keeps us more focused on criticisms than compliments, favoring bad news over good. Because we're so prone to going negative, keep the following points in mind as you work to build positivity.

Negativity is a force. Negativity and negative emotions aren't simply the absence of positivity. Negativity has a life and force of its own. Even a minor event, like a grouchy look from someone, a minor mistake we make at work, or being stuck in traffic for a few extra minutes, can spiral into a sense that everything is going wrong, with ourselves and with our world. These negative thought loops can take us into an ongoing negative emotional tone, as we dwell on regrets about the past, judge ourselves unworthy or unlovable, or blame others for our problems. These ruminative cycles build on themselves and gain power, like a snowball gathering momentum as it rolls down a hill.

Positive response: When a small moment of negativity occurs, use a mindfulness technique (for example, the open sky meditation on page 38 or the mindfulness meditation on page 85) to let negative thoughts drift away.

We can catch negativity from others. Negativity can spread from one person to another like a virus. We can find ourselves pulled into negativity not only because of our own thoughts, but because of something someone else says or does. When this pattern continues in the workplace or other group setting, it can be as if there's a vortex of negativity that draws people into the proverbial water cooler complaints about the boss or gossiping about what a coworker said or did.

> **Positive response:** If you can't gently steer a negative exchange in a positive direction, excuse yourself and move on before the negativity takes root.

Negativity is bad for your physical health. We discussed how positive emotions give your health a widespread boost. Negative emotions such as anger and fear have the opposite impact on the immune system and your health in general. Even a five-minute episode of anger causes an outpouring of stress hormones, making your heart beat faster and increasing your blood pressure.

> **Positive response:** Like Jake in the example on page 72, pay attention to signs that negative emotions are taking hold, like increased heart rate, shortness of breath, or feeling your body get tense or hot. Calm yourself with controlled breathing, blow off some steam by going for a walk, or do one of the meditation exercises in this book.

The Inner Critic

Perhaps the most problematic of all negative thought patterns is what's known as the *inner critic*. We all experience this voice in our heads: It's the one that's busy evaluating us, finding fault, and throwing insults at us for our actions and words. Our inner critic tells us things like:

You're not smart enough.

Why did you say that?

You'll never amount to anything.

You're a complete imposter.

You're going to blow this. You always do.

Often this inner critic is a mix of critical voices we've heard over the years from parents, teachers, siblings, coaches, and others, internalized and knit together into a painful chorus of personal inadequacy. Over time, the voice becomes so familiar that we may even believe it's our own. Because of feelings of shame around the abuse I endured, I developed an inner voice that said there was something deeply wrong with me, that I was different than other people, almost subhuman. From the way I walked to how I looked to almost everything I said, this harsh voice ran my life, limiting me in countless ways.

But voices like these are never true to the unfolding reality of who we are. Not for me and not for you. The inner critic's messages are based on selected snapshots, and inaccurate ones at that. They don't reflect the full story of who we are and what we do in all moments of our lives. The inner critic ignores our moments of tenderness, kindness, generosity, and goodwill that are also a part of our days. Nevertheless, that voice can be powerful, leaving us in what mindfulness educator Tara Brach, PhD, calls a *trance of unworthiness*. If we let the inner critic hold sway, we come to believe that we're defective, undeserving of the same kindness as others, belittled, unworthy, incompetent, and a disappointment.

No matter how authoritative these criticisms may seem, I can guarantee that they do not speak the truth of who you really are.

For positivity to take hold and resilience to deepen, we have to diminish that inner critic. We must see the critic for what it is: misguided. Once we do, we free ourselves from its reign. This is where mindfulness can powerfully help. As we bring our focus to the current moment and pay greater attention to what's truly happening in our inner world, we see that the inner critic is just a voice, typically one that does not speak the truth. We can see more and more clearly that though we're not perfect—nobody is—we're much less imperfect than our inner critic proclaims.

RESILIENCE PRACTICE:
Managing the Inner Critic

Negative thinking about ourselves, our circumstances, and those around us wears us down, depleting our resilience well and making it difficult for us to cope with the challenges in our lives. Use this exercise to free yourself from your inner negative voice.

Sit comfortably in a place where you can write without being disturbed. Record the answers in your journal or a notebook.

1. Write down a common critical and negative message you have about yourself.

2. Ask yourself:

    Is this message true?

    How do I know that it's true or false?

3. Notice how you feel when you experience this critical message. Which of the following describes your mood? Write down all that apply and add any other descriptors that are relevant.

    Down   Up

    Sad   Happy

    Worried   Free

4. When you experience the critical message, how does your body feel? Write down your answers.

    Heavy   Light

    Depleted   Energized

CONTINUED

5. Now push yourself to dispute the negative message. Write down at least one refutation of the message, phrasing it this way:

> One thing that tells me that this inner critic message is untrue is . . .

For example, if your critical message was "I can't get myself organized," your refuting statement might be "One thing that tells me that this inner critic message is untrue is that I always remember friends' birthdays and send them a card or gift."

6. Read over your refuting statement. Notice your mood and how your body feels, and rate them using the same descriptors. Has anything changed? Write a brief description of the difference.

This week, see if you can catch your inner critic in action. When you detect that negative internal voice, notice how you feel. Push yourself to ask whether the message is true. Then take the time to refute the message in at least one way. Doing this will help you see yourself in a more kind and realistic light.

Optimistic Outlook

The word optimism comes from the Latin *optimus*, meaning "best." An optimistic person looks for the best in situations and expects it to occur. Pessimists, on the other hand, see the worst in situations, sure that bad outcomes are the most likely. Where the optimist sees possibility, the pessimist sees dead ends. Put another way, a pessimist sees the difficulty in every opportunity; an optimist sees the opportunity in every difficulty.

Optimism is indisputably good for your resilience. Like positive emotions, optimism improves both physical health and life success. In a study involving 70,000 nurses, researchers found that higher optimism was associated with a lower risk of mortality from many major causes of death, including cancer, heart disease, and stroke. In another study, people with a family history of heart disease who also had a positive outlook were one-third less likely to have a heart attack than those with a more negative outlook. Another study found that optimistic people were 13 percent less likely than their negative counterparts to have a heart attack or other coronary event. In terms of life success, optimism has also been shown to correlate with better grades on exams, higher sales among insurance agents, and faster recovery from injury in athletes.

Thinking about optimism calls to mind the old saw of seeing a glass as half empty or half full. Shawn Achor, author of *The Happiness Advantage*, notes that it doesn't really matter whether the glass is half empty or half full; what matters is that we have a pitcher to refill it. That pitcher is our well of resilience. Per positive psychology, whether we're an optimist or a pessimist boils down to how we explain things to ourselves. In other words, when two people experience the same situation—let's say a presentation at work that leads to negative feedback—optimists and pessimists each tell themselves something very different.

First, the optimist tends to see the situation as temporary, telling themselves "I'll do better next time." A pessimist will decide on a more permanent explanation, such as "I'm terrible at giving presentations." Second, pessimists tend to generalize their self-criticism, concluding, "I'm not very smart" as opposed to an optimist's "I'm not good at these kind of things." Third, optimists see the impact of factors outside their control, whereas the pessimist internalizes the result with a sense of blame. The optimist might say, "I didn't have enough time to prepare." A pessimist could conclude, "Everyone else is so good at this. What's wrong with me?"

Clearly, our explanatory style—optimistic or pessimistic—impacts how we perceive our world and how we react to the stresses we experience. With an optimistic lens, we see possibility, thus we actively employ a wider range of problem-solving strategies and have a sense of hope regarding the outcome. Pessimism, like many negative emotions, narrows our focus and limits our sense of options. In an extreme form, pessimism can set us up for a state called *learned helplessness*, a belief that we can't improve our situation even when we can. By learning optimism instead, we can move from self-pity, resentment, and avoidance of problems to creativity in facing our struggles head on.

Do you consider yourself an optimist or a pessimist? Which way do you lean? You might think that either style of thinking is beyond your ability to change, but all of us can learn to exert control over our mind state and shift from pessimism to optimism. Returning to the image of our mind being like a garden, we can choose to water seeds of negativity or those of positivity. If we decide that things are always bound to turn out poorly, then our tendency toward fear and worry will take hold and grow stronger. If we engage in gratitude, and remind ourselves that things could always be worse, our optimism will grow.

RESILIENCE PRACTICE: Magic Monday

We've seen how important positive emotions and optimism are. Yet our minds are biased toward the negative, and for many of us negativity is comfortable and familiar. This exercise shows you how you can benefit from choosing to focus on the positive, even when things are difficult.

1. Sit quietly in a place where you won't be distracted. Close your eyes, get comfortable, and imagine that you're beginning your work week or your usual Monday routine. (We'll continue to use the workplace as our example, but you can substitute whatever situation reflects your own life.)

2. Imagine your workday this coming Monday. You'll go to your usual workplace and encounter all the usual people, tasks, and concerns. But one thing will be different: Throughout the day, you're focused on the

positives within yourself, in others, and in all the tasks and activities that fill your day.

3. Start with your commute: See, in your mind's eye, your usual trip to work. What will look different, or feel different, if you focus on the positive? Maybe you're stuck in the usual morning traffic crawl, but instead of frustration you focus on the faces of people in nearby cars and get curious about what their lives are like.

4. Now imagine your day at work. Picture the people you see in the hallway and around your workspace, everyone you interact with on a typical day. Imagine moving through a typical day's agenda and focus on seeing the positive in yourself and those you interact with. How does your positive outlook affect what you do, the conversations you have, and the choices you make? Perhaps you smile at the people you typically barely pay attention to, or even strike up a conversation.

5. Now imagine your end-of-day commute and who you interact with on your way home. You might stop at the gas station or the supermarket or share a carpool ride. What are your conversations like? Picture going into your home again with this positive vantage point. Imagine how you greet and interact with your family. Take in how you feel inside yourself. Complete this exercise by imagining getting into bed for the night, again focusing on the positives of your day. How do you feel as you drift off to sleep? Do you perhaps even have a different quality of sleep?

Did you notice differences compared to your usual workday? If so, what were they? If you'd like, write them down in your journal.

KEY TAKEAWAYS

■ After historically focusing on deficits, the field of human psychology now recognizes that focusing on strengths and positivity is vital for understanding optimal human functioning.

■ Positive emotions fuel problem-solving, creativity, and physical and mental health.

■ Negativity is more than the absence of positivity; a trivial negative event can gain momentum and overwhelm us. Other peoples' negativity can trigger our own.

■ Many of us suffer with a harsh inner critic sitting in judgment of our words, thoughts, and actions. But these negative messages rarely reflect the full truth of who we are.

■ With practice, we can silence the inner critic and see more clearly the reality of our many strengths and talents.

■ Whether we're an optimist or a pessimist boils down to how we explain things to ourselves.

■ We can learn to exert tremendous control over our mind state, changing our explanatory style to become more optimistic.

CHAPTER 7

Self-Care

If we don't tend to our own mental, physical, emotional, and spiritual well-being, who will? And yet most of us don't make self-care a priority. In fact, when life gets busy, very often it's the first thing to be dropped from our list of priorities. As a result, we can end up running on empty, our resilience drained. In this chapter we'll examine the reasons that we're lax in our self-care and explore some methods of replenishing your well of resilience by taking care of your own well-being.

Cultivate Self-Care

If you think about it, taking care of yourself is a pretty obvious strategy for building resilience. The healthier we are in body and mind, the better we can weather the stresses and difficulties that come our way. But many times we put care of ourselves on the back burner, again and again. We tell ourselves that we don't have time to make a healthy meal, that it would be self-indulgent to get more sleep, or that other things are more important than stretching our legs and getting some exercise. With so many obligations and responsibilities, and with so much that we want or need to get done, we can habitually put our own care last.

But the cost of doing that can be high: loss of compassion for others, burnout, and the downward spirals of depression and reduced productivity. If you're someone who lets their self-care slide, think about what happens when you're running on empty. Does your mood fall off? Do you become less efficient with tasks?

To make self-care a consistent priority, we need to vanquish some of the beliefs that keep us from looking after our wellness. Here are three common misconceptions to let go of:

I have other priorities. Yes, your life is likely busy, and you have many responsibilities. And you may have grown up with the belief that the more you sacrifice, the more successful you'll be. But regularly sacrificing care for your body and soul will leave you depleted. With your resilience weakened, it will be more difficult to achieve your goals and fulfill your obligations. Investing in yourself will enable you to handle your other priorities with greater ease.

I'm not worth it. For some of us, due to low self-worth, we feel less important than those around us, and as a result we take less care of ourselves than we should. This can become a vicious cycle; we struggle to put time into self-care, then find fault with ourselves for struggling, which confirms our low opinion of ourselves. Replacing that negative thinking with an upward spiral can be a game-changer: The more you engage in self-care, the more you'll feel that you are worth it, which then makes further self-care more doable. This is another way that putting aside self-blame in favor of self-compassion helps us be resilient.

I'm too busy. Maybe you'd like to put self-care at the top of your list, but your list is so long that there's not enough time for everything. To say yes to self-care, we often have to say no to competing demands on our time and energy. Consider all the things you believe you should be doing and question whether all of them are valid. You'll likely find that you can give up some of those "shoulds."

In the end, self-care is about more than just ourselves. When we engage in activities that promote our well-being, we're better able to care for others and meet all our responsibilities. Self-care has been shown to decrease stress in childcare workers, trauma therapists, physicians, nurses, and others who need to be at their best to care for others. You're probably familiar with the airline safety instruction that has become a metaphor for self-care: Put your own oxygen mask on first, so you can then help someone else put on theirs. Yet though self-care often involves a specific activity, sometimes it simply means not having to spend time being productive, just allowing oneself to rest, perhaps reading a good book or taking a nap.

Here's a story that illustrates the greater good that can come when we make self-care a priority.

> Mimi, an Asian American woman in her 50s, grew up with a mother who was mentally ill. Mimi was often the target of her mother's delusions. But Mimi was also the one who had to care for her mother during periods when she couldn't care for herself. These pressures led Mimi to develop severe depression as a teen, culminating in a hospitalization for attempted suicide. Afterward, she worked with a trusted therapist, found medication that eased her depression, and invested more time and energy in looking after her own well-being. Developing a greater ability to care for herself

enabled Mimi to escape her family's legacy of mental illness. As an adult she advocated for other Asian American women struggling with depression and became a speaker for a suicide-prevention organization. Doing so filled her well with a sense of meaning and purpose that fueled an upward cycle of greater self-care.

Now that we've seen the importance of self-care, it's time for you to follow through and take responsibility for looking after your own wellness. Here's an exercise to get you started.

RESILIENCE PRACTICE: Don't Run on Empty

Self-care isn't a one-size-fits-all process. We all have different ways of replenishing our bodies and minds. This exercise will create an inventory of self-care practices and help you decide where to put your energies. Record the answers in your journal.

1. Sit comfortably in a place where you can write without interruption. Spend a few minutes reflecting on what's going on in your life. Think about times when you're at your busiest and moments when things slow down and you have time to breathe.

2. Write down your answers to these questions:

    What are the small things in your life that help you feel strong and solid?

    What nourishes you?

    What brings you comfort?

If you have trouble answering, think about these examples. Which resonate with you? What else would you add to the list?

Taking a hot bath

Exercising

Making time to be with a friend or family member

Listening to your favorite music

Reading a book

Taking a walk

Being outside in nature

Having a hot cup of tea

3. Now consider what activities you're not currently doing, or don't do often, which would bring you strength, nourishment, and comfort. List at least three.

Examples:

- Joining a support group for people with similar challenges
- Letting yourself have a good cry
- Taking a class or workshop on a subject that interests you
- Forgiving yourself for something you regret
- Exploring a new or existing hobby
- Working in your garden

CONTINUED

4. Next, ask yourself what activities you can give up, or do less of, in the name of self-care. List at least three.

Examples:

- Repeatedly watching or reading news reports that upset you
- Spending time around negative people
- Using television, social media, or Internet time to avoid difficult emotions or loneliness
- Reaching for substances to get away from emotional pain

5. Review the list of activities you've compiled. For each, write down one step you can take to incorporate or eliminate it.

Examples:

> "Make a cup of tea each morning and enjoy it for ten minutes with my phone turned off."

> "Spend most Saturday mornings at the park instead of going to the mall."

> "Check the community college website to see what evening classes are starting next month."

Once you've done this exercise, perhaps you can add new activities to your schedule, blocking off time on your calendar or setting a reminder alarm until they become part of your regular routine. It takes practice to avoid running on empty, but that practice is well worth the gain.

Practice Self-Compassion

At various points in this book, we've touched on the importance of being kind to ourselves, of turning off self-judgment and replacing it with self-compassion. In chapter 6, we discussed how our inner critic can be one loud and mean inner bully. How can we overcome the trials and hardships of the outside world if we're constantly attacking ourselves on the inside? We can learn to quiet this inner force and stand up to ourselves just as we would to an outer bully. Self-compassion is imperative for building resilience.

Many of us are in the habit of being very harsh with ourselves. We say things to ourselves that we would never say to anyone else, least of all to someone we care about. To build a habit of self-compassion, we first need to reflect on what compassion is: seeing suffering and being moved to alleviate it.

Imagine seeing a frail elderly woman carrying bags of groceries, struggling to cross the street, looking overburdened and forlorn. Picture that in your mind's eye. Notice how you feel. Perhaps there's a sense of your mood softening as you see her struggle, along with a desire to help. What likely occurred for you is a three-step process:

- Awareness that suffering is occurring
- Having an emotional response to it
- Feeling a common humanity with the person suffering, a "there but for the grace of God go I" sentiment

With self-compassion, we turn that same process toward ourselves. We see that *we* are the one suffering. With the same compassion we bring to others, we are moved to alleviate our own suffering, and we're reminded that suffering is the lot of all humans.

One way to understand self-compassion is to shine a light on self-criticism and why it often makes things more difficult for us. When we're critical of ourselves, we're triggering our brain's threat and defense system, that high-alert, fight/flight/freeze reaction discussed in chapter 1. In this case, the source of the "attack" is ourselves, as we judge ourselves so harshly that it actually feels like a threat. And with stress hormones flooding our bodies, we don't perform any better on the task at hand. Instead, we may find ourselves paralyzed by anxiety and procrastination.

Self-compassion, on the other hand, triggers a very different response, sometimes called the *tend and befriend* system, which puts us on the best footing to learn and grow. When applied to ourselves, compassion builds what we might consider an inner ally or caregiver.

What Self-Compassion Is Not

When you hear the term "self-compassion," does it sound like something that's for softies? Do you find that self-compassion carries connotations of being selfish or seems like a form of self-pity? If the concept is new to you, you might have the idea that self-compassion will make you lazy, that you'll somehow devolve into slothful inactivity if you don't drive yourself with self-criticism.

These are common misconceptions about self-compassion. In truth, it's not just another way of saying "poor me." Instead, self-compassion declares: *There's suffering here. What can I do to alleviate it?* And when you choose to practice self-compassion, it's not only you that benefits. It turns out that only through kindness toward ourselves are we most motivated to achieve our goals and support others.

The Benefits of Self-Compassion

The science of self-compassion supports its importance in replenishing our well of resilience. A large body of studies by self-compassion researcher and author Kristin Neff, PhD, and others shows that people who are high in self-compassion respond less strongly to negative events, cope better with difficult situations like divorce, experience less fear of failure, and have greater overall life satisfaction. Studies have also confirmed that self-compassion brings benefits to our physical health, including decreased chronic-pain severity, decreased alcohol consumption, and increased regular exercise.

For myself and for the physicians and nurses I coach, I've seen over and over the detrimental impact of self-criticism, and how self-kindness actually improves one's ability to work productively, increasing a sense of joy in caring for patients and providing resilience to the pressures of the work. If you're a caregiver in your work or at home, it's important to understand that your compassion for others doesn't automatically translate to compassion for yourself. Sometimes our heart is open to others but tightly closed to ourselves, generating a sense of separation from those around us. It's as if we're saying that others are worthy of compassion and we're not. Over time, this depletes our inner well of resilience and contributes to burnout and exhaustion.

Sometimes we find ourselves questioning why difficulties are happening to us. We feel like something has gone wrong when life doesn't go the way we want it to. With self-compassion, we begin to recognize we shouldn't find fault with ourselves because our life isn't perfect... because no one's life is perfect or without suffering. With that realization, we can come to a greater feeling of connection to others, as opposed to feeling isolated or isolating ourselves—something we tend to do when we feel inadequate.

RESILIENCE PRACTICE:
Take a Self-Compassion Break

Though self-care is critically important, many self-care practices are done apart from our time at our jobs and other responsibilities. But self-compassion is a form of self-care we can access at any time, and it's particularly important to call on it during moments of difficulty. For most of us, it takes practice to build our ability to treat ourselves with compassion. This self-compassion break, first developed by Kristin Neff, PhD, is intended to stop cascading voices of doubt and self-criticism.

CONTINUED

1. Think of a situation that is challenging and causing you stress. Call the situation to mind. Take a moment and see if you can actually feel the stress and emotional discomfort in your body.

2. Put your right hand over your heart, feeling its warmth and gentle pressure on your chest. Say these words to yourself:

   > This is a moment of suffering. This is hard. This is how it feels when someone is going through what I'm going through. Suffering is part of life for all of us.

3. Now say the following to yourself:

   > *May I be kind to myself in this moment.*
   > *May I give myself the compassion I need*
   > *and deserve.*
   > *May I forgive myself in whatever ways*
   > *will help me.*
   > *May I accept that I'm an imperfect human*
   > *among other imperfect humans.*

If you find it difficult to direct compassion toward yourself in this way, imagine that a good friend or loved one is going through what you're going through. What would you say to them?

Take a moment to reflect on how this exercise made youfeel. If it felt uncomfortable, that's likely because you're used to being less than kind to yourself. As you go through your week, keep taking regular self-compassion breaks. The more you use this exercise, the easier self-compassion will come to you.

Scheduling "Me Time"

Making time for yourself can be a challenge. But the cost of not doing so is high. Here's an example of how a choice to take time for one's self can be the best thing even when it's difficult to do.

> Hilde was spending most of her waking hours caring for her husband, Richard, who had begun developing Alzheimer's disease four years earlier. After so many years, she was exhausted from taking care of him around the clock. But she felt that taking time for herself would be selfish—after all, she wasn't the one with the illness. So she continued to spend almost all of her time tending to his needs.
>
> Then Hilde's own health began to suffer. She realized that if she didn't do something, she'd end up not only sick, but also unable to care for Richard at all. She consulted with her children, who encouraged her to hire an in-home care-giver. Soon she had time every day when she could catch her breath, go for a walk, and focus on matters important to her. Her health improved and she was able to manage the demands of Richard's illness much more effectively.

Sometimes scheduling time for ourselves means we have to let go of a sense of control over things. We have to give up a belief that if we aren't the one handling something, it won't get done as well as we'd like. Or that we're the only one who can get the job done. For Hilde, self-care meant entrusting Richard's care to someone else, something that did not come easily for her. Yet she knew that if she didn't share the burden, soon she'd be unable to carry it at all.

Self-Care Priorities

One of the keys to self-care is scheduling time for it. When we don't, everything else becomes the priority and care for ourselves falls off. Sometimes we look at our schedule and see appointment after appointment, time spent at work or meeting the needs of others. Putting yourself on your schedule signifies making the same commitment to yourself. And though self-care options are many, let's look at a few important ones.

Exercise is a self-care activity that brings many benefits. On the physical health front, weight loss, blood pressure control, decreased risk of stroke, improved insomnia, and lowered risk of Alzheimer's disease are but a few of the benefits of getting regular exercise. Regarding mental health, exercise decreases both depression and anxiety, reduces levels of stress hormones, and increases energy levels. And in terms of brain health, exercise improves memory, promotes the brain's ability to form new neural connections, and reduces brain inflammation. With thousands of studies backing up the positive impact of exercise, the benefits are unequivocal. Schedule exercise time on your calendar and consider those appointments as important as any work meeting or other obligation. And try to include physical activity as part of every day, like going for a walk or doing work around the house or garden.

Nutrition is too vast to do justice to here. Generally speaking, a diet low in saturated fat, with minimal sugary beverages and multiple daily servings of fruit and vegetables, will support your health. Your doctor or a nutritionist can help you plan a diet that meets your particular needs. Suffice it to say that whether it's eating a diet high in unsaturated fat, avoiding sugary beverages, or being sure to include multiple daily servings of fruit and vegetables, good nutritional choices will contribute to your resilience.

Adequate sleep brings numerous physical and mental health benefits. Many studies reveal that insufficient sleep increases the risk of developing serious medical conditions, from obesity and diabetes to Alzheimer's disease to a shortened lifespan. Though it can be tempting to trade sleep for time to get more done, the time you save will be offset by your fatigue, difficulty concentrating, and poorer performance. Some of us require eight solid hours and others only six to seven. Pay attention to how much sleep you need to feel rested, and sleep on a consistent schedule.

Meditation, a self-care strategy that's not as familiar as exercise or healthy eating, can confer widespread health benefits. For the brain, meditation decreases the size of the amygdala and increases the thickness of the gray matter in the prefrontal cortex—the part of the brain involved in complex thought—and other key areas. Meditation also decreases blood pressure, lowers risk of heart disease and stroke, and decreases risk of recurrence of major depression. Just as important, meditation brings us to the present moment where we are typically safer and more okay than in a mythical future, taking us out of the fear, worry, and anxiety we can all drift into. If you don't have an existing meditation practice, try the open sky meditation (page 38) and the mindfulness meditation (page 85) in this book.

Not sure where to start? Quality is often more important that quantity here, as even the smallest act of self-care reverses patterns and beliefs that can get in our way. For myself, making self-care a priority started with committing to enjoying a cup of tea every afternoon. This sounds so small, yet it was a vital step in allowing myself to feel worthy of self-care. Let's look at some tips to help you build your self-care habits.

RESILIENCE PRACTICE:
Making Self-Care a Reality

We can tell ourselves that we can't fit self-care into our schedule and consider everyone and everything else more important. Here are a few tips to ensure that self-care occurs.

Schedule time for yourself. If it's not scheduled, it likely won't happen. Think about periods during your day and week when you are most confident that you can set aside time for self-care. Whether you use a paper or digital calendar, be sure to include your "me time" on it. Block time on shared calendars so others will know you're unavailable. And just as you wouldn't cancel a medical appointment with short notice, don't cancel on yourself.

Make it standard. Creating a mini-ritual can help you make sure that self-care occurs. Perhaps when you get home from work, you can take 10 minutes for something pleasurable before you do anything else. Or spend 10 minutes meditating or taking a hot bath before bed every night, as part of your pre-sleep routine. The more you integrate self-care with your other daily activities, the more readily it will become your habit.

Set a goal. Are you someone who likes to set a goal and check off your wins? This is a tried-and-true method for keeping on track. Set a goal for things like exercise (number of miles walked per week), meditation, and getting to bed on time (how often can you do it?). Once achieved, give yourself the pleasure of checking it off: milestone reached!

Consider a technology break. Many of us have become slaves to our technology, almost constantly attending to texts, emails, and alerts. As difficult as this can be, try establishing regular no-screen times, when you put away your devices to sit quietly and think, get some exercise, prepare a healthy meal, or be more present with loved ones.

Start small. Don't feel like you have to transform your self-care habits all at once. If you're not used to taking time for yourself, whatever you can do is a great start. If you get off track, don't berate yourself, just start again.

Perhaps my own motto can be helpful:

> *When you start something new, start very small.*
> *That's much better than not starting at all.*

KEY TAKEAWAYS

- Self-care helps keep your mind and body primed to deal with situations that require resilience.

- When we put ourselves last, the cost can be high—loss of compassion for others and the downward spirals of depression and loss of productivity.

- To make self-care a consistent priority, we need to give up the belief that we're not worth it and say no to competing demands on our time and energy that keep us from looking after our wellness.

- Self-compassion means treating ourselves as kindly as we treat our friends or others we care about.

- To make sure that you engage in self-care, it's important to put it on your schedule.

- Exercise, good nutrition, adequate sleep, and meditation have significant physical, mental, and brain-health benefits and each helps fill your resilience well.

CHAPTER 8

Resilience for Life

Whether you've been working through this book chapter by chapter or creating your own path based on your particular needs, you've taken a tremendous step forward in building your resilience. You've chosen to invest in yourself, expending time and energy to learn new strategies and try out new tools. That's not always an easy decision given all the distractions and pressures that demand our attention. Going forward, I hope you will return to this book as often as you need to, whether it's to refresh your skills, deepen your understanding, or teach yourself an exercise that you'd passed over.

Moving Forward

Know that you're in charge of your journey. Whatever course you follow in cultivating and strengthening your resilience, the key concepts we've discussed will continue to help and guide you. Perhaps the most important one to remember is that though we tend to think of resilience as something exhibited by heroes and those with superpowers, in truth it's a quality that you have within you, and always have. I've shared many real-life stories of people struggling with issues small and large, and examples of how they coped with challenge and adversity. You've heard my own story, which I've shared because I want you to know that no matter what you experience in your life, you are still resilient. This is true for all of us.

What this book has provided are the tools and knowledge that can help you access and replenish your well on a regular basis. Resilience is your well of inner resourcefulness that allows you to sustain yourself through whatever difficulties and challenges you encounter. It's strengthened by connection, flexibility, perseverance, self-regulation, positivity, and self-care. When you attend to your resilience by cultivating those attributes, you'll be capable of shifting any difficult situation in your life from overwhelming to manageable.

As you travel onward toward everyday resilience, here are some practices that will ensure your success:

Rely on mindfulness. The practice of mindfulness is extremely helpful in cultivating resilience. As we first discussed in chapter 3, mindfulness means paying attention to your thoughts, your emotions, and your bodily sensations, in the present moment. The more you leave mental stories and pay attention to what's real and true in your current experience, the more you'll become aware of what you need to do to be resilient. You'll notice when your body is telling you that something is off—like when your shoulders are tight or your heart is racing or you're yawning away in need of rest. If you're new to mindfulness, be sure to use the open sky meditation (page 38) and the mindfulness meditation (page 85) as often as you can. I encourage you to explore mindfulness further, at your own pace; see the resource list at the end of this book (page 129) for suggestions.

Employ self-compassion. None of us are perfect, yet we're all much more okay than we often realize. Our inborn negativity bias leads us to focus on our faults and the things that we don't do well, so be on guard against this tendency. Revisit chapters 6 and 7 whenever it becomes difficult to focus on what's good about yourself and your actions. Don't let your inner critic derail your efforts to develop everyday resilience. And remember that directing compassion to yourself enables you to be compassionate and helpful to others in your life.

Focus on the positive. As discussed in chapter 1, our malleable brains are constantly developing new neural pathways based on our experiences and what we focus on. What you direct your attention toward can truly become your reality, as your brain creates connections and networks that support those thoughts. Dwell on your positive experiences and successes, and your brain will become more inclined to focus on these. Whenever you can let go of negativity in the form of grudges, anger, or resentments, you'll grow your ability to be more positive. This positivity creates an upward spiral of growth and efficacy that actively replenishes your well of resilience. When you're finding positivity particularly hard to hold on to, turn to the Magic Monday practice in chapter 6.

Make connections. Reading a book is a fairly solitary pursuit, so it bears mentioning again that the more you can lean into connecting with other people, the more your resilience will grow. Humans are a highly social species, so don't underestimate how vital the encouragement, validation, reassurance, and support that we receive through our social connections are for our well-being. Whether through micro-moments or deep relationships—hopefully both—developing and maintaining connection is a lifeline for getting through difficult times. Some of us are more naturally social than others, so call on the practices outlined in chapter 2 if you need help making and deepening connections.

Remember the three marks. Finally, in times of difficulty, I hope you will bring to mind the three marks of existence that we covered in chapter 3. Contemplating these truths can be revelatory when you're feeling overwhelmed by hardships. The first mark is that bad things happen and suffering occurs. This is true for all of us. The second is that things are always changing and nothing is permanent. And the third is that little in life is truly personal. Though we might wish otherwise, these truths can be a grounding and steadying force. When you keep them in mind, you will likely experience far less suffering from that second arrow (also in chapter 3).

Staying the Course

Resilience is an ongoing process, not a one-time decision or action. It's something we build continually with the many life choices we make in the course of our days. There are innumerable choice points in our lives, and every one can add to our resilience. And when it doesn't, don't worry; there are always more choices coming up. Here are two pitfalls to avoid along the way:

Comparing your situation to someone else's. Even when our overall movement is forward, little in life is linear. There will be times when you're true to yourself and your purpose, and times when you aren't. That's simply the nature of life. We all walk our own path to resilience, with unique twists and turns, loops and abrupt reversals. Though we can expend a lot of mental energy comparing ourselves to others, keep in mind the often-quoted saying: "Comparisons are the thief of joy." In other words, comparisons with how others live their lives just lead to discontent. Your resilience depends on keeping comparisons in check.

Putting your self-care last. I'm confident that you can invest in your resilience every day. We all feel the pressure to put self-care on the back burner, but I want to encourage you not to do so. If we don't keep our well of resilience replenished by attending to our well-being, we'll find it wanting at those times when we need it most. However busy your days become, take a careful look at your schedule and be sure to plan for self-care every single day, even if it's a small moment of calm on a hectic to-do list. Make that investment in your well-being. And if it sometimes feels selfish to prioritize your own care, remember that you can't care for anyone else if you don't care for yourself. No matter what your responsibilities and how many balls you're juggling, know that you are truly worth every act of self-care.

Final Thoughts

I hope spending time with this book gives you a sense of confidence in your ability to meet the challenges you face, and in your ability to live in a way that contributes to your sense of purpose and vitality. I also hope you experience a healthy sense of control over your life and your growing resilience has you feeling less blown about by the winds of fate and less at the mercy of whatever comes in your path. Please know that resilience is your birthright. We are each born with a full inner well of resilience, a core of strength and goodness that can buffer us in times of difficulty. My goal with this book is to help you see this more clearly, so you can tap into your inner resources more readily and more consistently.

In closing, I want to remind you that while none of us can go back and write a new beginning, we can all write a new ending. We can't change the challenges and traumatic events we've endured. We can't change the family we were born into. We can't change how we or others acted in the past. But we can all begin, today, to write a new ending for our life story. We are truly the authors of our lives. And knowing that, my dear reader, is what will make you resilient.

Resources

Chapter 1

Altered Traits: Science Reveals How Meditation Changes Your Mind, Brain, and Body, by Daniel Goleman and Richard J. Davidson (Penguin, 2017)
One of most thorough collections of research on mindfulness and meditation available.

"Understanding the Stress Response," by Harvard Health, Health.Harvard.edu/staying-healthy/understanding-the -stress-response
An excellent resource for understanding the fight/flight/freeze physiology and neuroanatomy.

"Neuroplasticity and Clinical Practice: Building Brain Power for Health" by Joyce Shaffer (*Frontiers in Psychology*, 2016)
A solid overview of the emerging research on neuroplasticity.

Chapter 2

Love 2.0: Finding Happiness and Health in Moments of Connection, by Barbara Fredrickson (Penguin, 2013)
This accessible read provides the science and practical wisdom on positive emotions with an emphasis on the foundational importance of love in optimal human functioning.

The Empathy Effect: Seven Neuroscience-Based Keys for Transforming the Way We Live, Love, Work, and Connect across Differences, by Helen Reiss (Sounds True Publishing, 2018)
A heartfelt and neuroscience-based overview of empathy by one of the world's leading empathy researchers.

Random Acts, RandomActs.org
A nonprofit organization and website providing resources on random acts of kindness.

VolunteerMatch, VolunteerMatch.org
A site devoted to matching individuals and volunteer opportunities.

Chapter 3

The Heart of the Buddha's Teaching: Transforming Suffering into Peace, Joy, and Liberation, by Thich Nhat Hanh (Rider, 1998)
A relatively easy read by one of the most revered mindfulness educators in the world, this book provides a thorough introduction to Buddhist philosophy and practices.

Mindfulness for Beginners: Reclaiming the Present Moment—and Your Life, by Jon Kabat-Zinn (Sounds True, 2012)
An easy-to-read primer on mindfulness from one of the leaders in the field.

Mindful Magazine, Mindful.org/magazine
An online and print magazine featuring articles and blog posts on many aspects of mindfulness and meditation.

Mindfulness-Based Stress Reduction Course
Developed by Jon Kabat-Zinn, this course is offered in person and online by healthcare facilities and community organizations across the globe, providing a wonderful foundation for exploring mindfulness.

Insight Timer, InsightTimer.com
A free app that offers thousands of guided meditations by leaders in the field of mindfulness.

Chapter 4

Grit: The Power of Passion and Perseverance, by Angela Duckworth (Simon and Schuster, 2016)
The seminal book on the role of perseverance in achieving life goals and happiness.

Helping People Change: Coaching with Compassion for Lifelong Learning and Growth, by Richard Boyatzis, Melvin L. Smith, and Ellen Van Oosten (Harvard Business Press, 2019)
A practical book that summarizes research on the intentional change theory and looks at inspiring people to reach their goals by connecting them to their most positive vision of themselves.

Goal Setting: A Scientific Guide to Setting and Achieving Goals, by James Clear, JamesClear.com/goal-setting
Excellent tips on goal setting by the author of *Atomic Habits: An Easy & Proven Way to Build Good Habits & Break Bad Ones* (Avery, 2018).

Chapter 5

Emotional Intelligence: Why It Can Matter More Than IQ, by Daniel Goleman (Bantam, 1995)
A foundational examination of emotional intelligence.

Radical Compassion: Learning to Love Yourself and Your World with the Practice of RAIN, by Tara Brach (Viking Life, 2019)
An easy-to-read book that explains the importance of compassion and self-compassion for individuals and for the health of the planet.

Fear: Essential Wisdom for Getting through the Storm, by Thich Nhat Hanh (Random House, 2012)
An excellent light read that provides a path for managing fear with wisdom and compassion.

Chapter 6

The University of Pennsylvania Positive Psychology Center,
   PPC.SAS.UPenn.edu
   This site provides comprehensive information on research,
   educational opportunities, and other resources about positive
   psychology.

*The Happiness Advantage: The Seven Principles of Positive Psychology
   That Fuel Success and Performance at Work*, by Shawn Achor (Crown
   Business, 2011)
   An excellent overview of positive psychology.

Chapter 7

Self-Care Resource Center, APA.org/helpcenter/self-care
   The American Psychological Association's site devoted to resources
   on self-care.

Self-Compassion, Self-Compassion.org
   Kristin Neff's site provides a thorough list of research, practices, and
   resources on self-compassion.

Chapter 8

The Greater Good Science Center, UC Berkeley, GreaterGood.Berkeley.edu
A carefully curated collection of research and other resources on resilience and living well.

The Mindful Way through Depression: Freeing Yourself from Chronic Unhappiness, by Mark Williams, John Teasdale, Zindel Segal, and Jon Kabat-Zinn (Guilford Press, 2007)
An excellent workbook that follows the evidence-based Mindfulness-Based Cognitive Therapy program for moving out of depression and anxiety.

References

Achor, Shawn. *The Happiness Advantage: The Seven Principles of Positive Psychology That Fuel Success and Performance at Work.* New York: Crown Business, 2010.

Berlin, Lisa, Yair Ziv, Lisa Amaya-Jackson, and Mark Greenberg. *Enhancing Early Attachments: Theory, Research, Intervention, and Policy.* New York: Guilford Press, 2007.

Boyatzis, Richard, Melvin L. Smith, and Ellen Van Oosten. *Helping People Change: Coaching with Compassion for Lifelong Learning and Growth.* Boston: Harvard Business School Press, 2019.

Brach, Tara. *Radical Compassion: Learning to Love Yourself and Your World with the Practice of RAIN.* New York: Penguin Random House, 2019.

Buchanan, Kathryn E., and Anat Bardi. "Acts of Kindness and Acts of Novelty Affect Life Satisfaction." *The Journal of Social Psychology* 150, no. 3 (2010): 235–37.

Duarte, Joana, and José Pinto-Gouveia. "Positive Affect and Parasympathetic Activity: Evidence for a Quadratic Relationship between Feeling Safe and Content and Heart Rate Variability." *Psychiatry Research* 257 (2017): 284–89.

Duckworth, Angela. *Grit: The Power of Passion and Perseverance.* New York: Simon and Schuster, 2016.

Fredrickson, Barbara. *Love 2.0: Finding Happiness and Health in Moments of Connection.* New York: Penguin, 2013

Goleman, Daniel. *Emotional Intelligence: Why It Can Matter More Than IQ.* New York: Bantam, 1995.

Hanh, Thich Nhat. *Taming the Tiger Within: Meditations on Transforming Difficult Emotions.* London: Penguin, 2004.

Harvard Health. "From Irritated to Enraged: Anger's Toxic Effect on the Heart." Published December 2014. Health.Harvard.edu/heart-health /from-irritated-to-enraged-angers-toxic-effect-on-the-heart.

Harvard Health. "Understanding the Stress Response." Published May 1, 2018. Health.Harvard.edu/staying-healthy/understanding-the-stress -response.

Hayes, Steven, with Spencer Smith. *Get Out of Your Mind and Into Your Life: The New Acceptance and Commitment Therapy.* Oakland: New Harbinger Publications, 2005.

Hotermans, Christophe, Philippe Peigneux, Alain Maertens De Noordhout, Gustave Moonen, and Pierre Maquet. "Repetitive Transcanial Magnetic Stimulation over the Primary Motor Cortex Disrupts Early Boost but Not Delayed Gains in Performance in Motor Sequence Learning." *European Journal of Neuroscience* 28, no. 6 (2008): 1216–21.

Hyde, Catherine Ryan. *Pay It Forward.* New York: Simon and Schuster, 2014.

Institute for Mindful Leadership. "Institute for Mindful Leadership." Accessed February 16, 2020. InstituteforMindfulLeadership.org.

The International Center for Self Care Research. "International Center for Self Care Research." Accessed March 20, 2020. SelfCareResearch.org.

Kim, Eric S., Kaitlin A. Hagan, Francine Grodstein, Dawn L. DeMeo, Immaculata De Vivo, and Laura D. Kubzansky. "Optimism and Cause-Specific Mortality: A Prospective Cohort Study." *American Journal of Epidemiology* 185, no. 1 (2017): 21–29.

Kuhn, C .M., and E. M. Flanagan. "Self-Care as a Professional Imperative: Physician Burnout, Depression, and Suicide." *Canadian Journal of Anaesthesia* 64 (2017): 158–168

The Mayo Clinic. "Chronic Stress Puts Your Health at Risk." Published May 19, 2019. Accessed February 27, 2020. MayoClinic.org/healthy -lifestyle/stress-management/in-depth/stress/art-20046037.

Neff, Kristin. "Self-Compassion Publications." Accessed January 16, 2020. Self-Compassion.org/the-research.

Niitsu, Kosuke, Michael J. Rice, Julia F. Houfek, Scott F. Stoltenberg, Kevin A. Kupzyk, and Cecilia R. Barron. "A Systematic Review of Genetic Influence on Psychological Resilience." *Biological Research for Nursing* 21, no. 1 (2019): 61–71.

Pattakos, Alex. *Prisoners of Our Thoughts: Viktor Frankl's Principles for Discovering Meaning in Life and Work*. With Foreword by Stephen R. Covey. San Francisco: Berrett-Koehler, 2008.

Rein, Glen, Mike Atkinson, and Rollin McCraty. "The Physiological and Psychological Effects of Compassion and Anger." *Journal of Advancement in Medicine* 8, no. 2 (1995): 87–105.

Riegel, Barbara, Sandra B. Dunbar, Donna Fitzsimons, Kenneth E. Freedland, Christopher S. Lee, Sandy Middleton, Anna Stromberg, Ercole Vellone, David E. Webber, and Tiny Jaarsma. "Self-Care Research: Where Are We Now? Where Are We Going?" *International Journal of Nursing Studies* (in press). doi.org/10.1016/j.ijnurstu.2019 .103402.

Riess, Helen. *The Empathy Effect: Seven Neuroscience-Based Keys for Transforming the Way We Live, Love, Work, and Connect across Differences*. Louisville: Sounds True Publishing, 2018.

Rogers, Carl. *On Becoming a Person: A Therapist's Version of Psychotherapy.* Boston: Houghton Mifflin, 1961.

Ryan, Richard M., and Edward L. Deci. "Self-Determination Theory and the Facilitation of Intrinsic Motivation, Social Development, and Well-Being." *American Psychologist* 55, no. 1 (2000): 68–78.

Sin, Nancy L., and Sonja Lyubomirsky. "Enhancing Well-Being and Alleviating Depressive Symptoms with Positive Psychology Interventions: A Practice-Friendly Meta-Analysis." *Journal of Clinical Psychology* 65, no. 5 (2009): 467–87.

Valtorta, Nicole K., Mona Kanaan, Simon Gilbody, Sara Ronzi, and Barbara Hanratty. "Loneliness and Social Isolation as Risk Factors for Coronary Heart Disease and Stroke: Systematic Review and Meta-Analysis of Longitudinal Observational Studies." *Heart* 102, no. 13 (2016): 1009–16.

Index

Acknowledgments

This book would not be where it is without the assistance of a number of key people. First, Carol Kauffman, dear friend and resilience guide, has been a key presence on my healing journey. Deep appreciation must be expressed for Beatrice Stipek, who was a patient and expert reader of early drafts. I'd also like to thank Liz Drance, Pata Suyemoto, and Susan Douthwaite for their help in this endeavor. Special thanks go to the wonderful editors at Callisto Media who have been a pleasure and a gift to work with. My understanding of resilience has been shaped by the many individuals who have made discovery in human psychology and mindfulness their life's work. Tara Brach, Jack Kornfield, Sharon Salzberg, Jon Kabat-Zinn, Thich Nhat Hanh, and Pema Chodron have been key teachers and I greatly appreciate them all. I also want to acknowledge my son, Daavi Gazelle, for his patience with me as his one and only parent. I mostly want to acknowledge the many patients and families who allowed me to participate in their sacred end-of-life journeys, and the physician coaching clients who have shared their vulnerability with so much honesty and integrity.

About the Author

 Gail Gazelle, MD, is a physician of 30 years, a Harvard Medical School part-time assistant professor, and a Master Certified Coach. A certified mindfulness teacher, she integrates neuroscience, mindfulness practices, and emotional intelligence to help people thrive and combat burnout. She is the author of the Harvard Health Guide *Mindfulness Support for Alzheimer's Caregivers*, and her innovative work has been featured by NPR, ABC, CNN, *O: The Oprah Magazine*, and the *New England Journal of Medicine*. Gail lives in Boston with her son and German Shepherd-Lab mix.

CPSIA information can be obtained
at www.ICGtesting.com
Printed in the USA
JSHW031650221021
19754JS00002B/10